Arusha
Poems & Essays

by

Lee McQueen

McQueen♟Press

2nd Edition [Includes two additional poems, repagination, and a new cover]

"Silk and Silver" [by Lee McQueen, *Sudan: The Lion of Truth*, 2nd ed, McQueen Press, 2011.]

"Breakaway" [by Lee McQueen, *Windrunner*, McQueen Press, 2012.]

"Reverie" [by Lee McQueen, *Road Romance: Tales from the Book Tour*, McQueen Press, 2013]

"The Ship of Fools" [by Lee McQueen, The *Dark Fantastic: 12 Short Screenplays*, McQueen Press, 2013.]

"Dreams in Arkana" [by Lee McQueen, *The Cadis Evening*, McQueen Press, 2016.]

"Writing Influences" [by Lee McQueen, *McQueen Press YouTube Channel*, 2016]

"My Sweet Baby" [by Lee McQueen, *Tamerlane,* (unpublished), 2019.]

"The Mountains Reach" [by Lee McQueen, *I Disappear: 3 Short Screenplays*, McQueen Press, 2020]

"Darica Lion 07168." [By Nevit Dilmen. *Wikipedia Commons.* 2007. Used with permission.]

Publisher's Catalog-in-Publication

McQueen, Lee, 1970-
Arusha: Poems & Essays/Lee McQueen
p. cm.
ISBN 978-1-7352369-3-3
    1. Poems
    2. Essays
I. Title

For the Ones who still believe in Tomorrow

Works by Lee McQueen

Short Story Collection

Imaginarium

Poetry Collection

Things I Forgot to Tell You

Novels

Kenzi

Celara Sun

Windrunner

The Cadis Evening

Screenplays

Kindred

SUDAN: The Lion of Truth

The Dark Fantastic: 12 Short Screenplays

I Disappear: 3 Short Screenplays

Non-Fiction

Writer in the Library! 41 Writers Reveal How They Use
Libraries to Develop Their Skill, Craft & Careers

Road Romance: Tales From the Book Tour

Man did not make this World.
Man cannot break this World.

Because of its mobility, the Black Queen is the most powerful player in the game.

Table of Contents

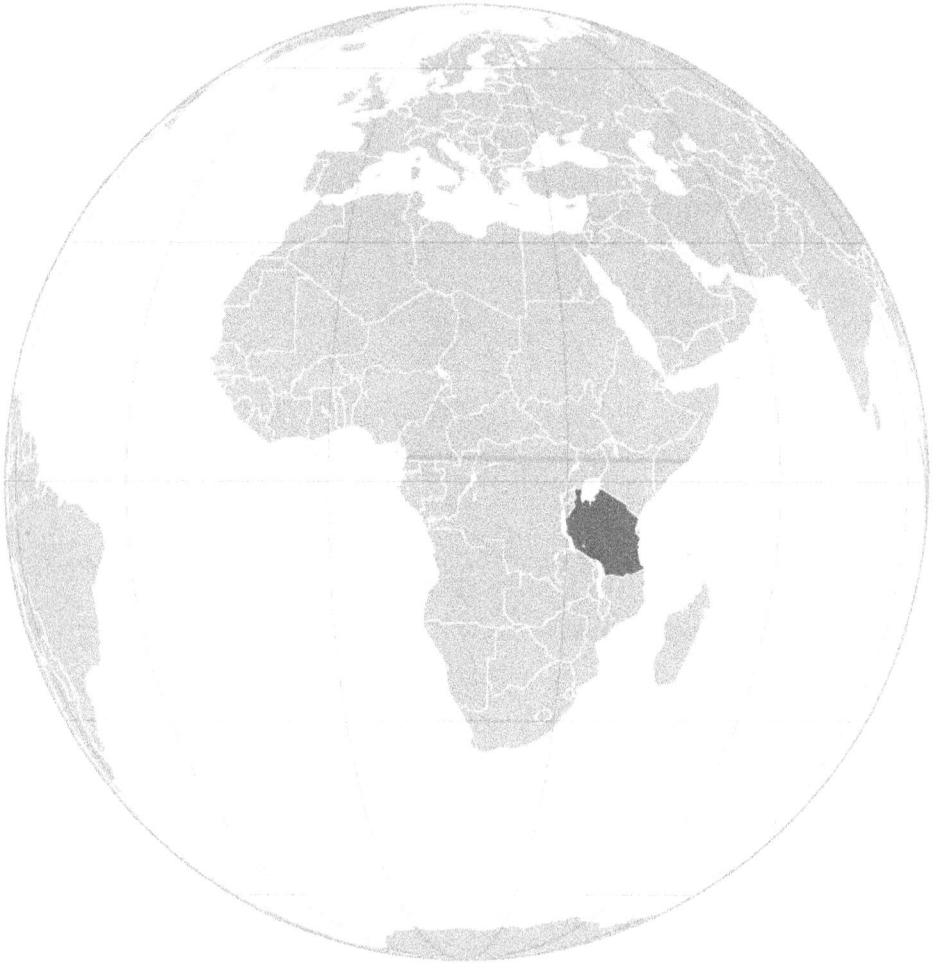

"Tanzania orthographic projection map" released to worldwide public domain by creator Marcos Elias de Oliveira Júnior, 19 June 2011.

Introduction

When life hands you lemons, you paint that shit gold. Many residents of the United States who traveled outside their borders for a vacation against racial, socio-political, and economic violence in 2020 brought gold spray paint, glitter, confetti, and ribbons with which to bedazzle their lemons.

Africa called me, I answered.

On my own journey, I turned towards the unknown, which meant either adventure and excitement or disaster and consequence.

So, faced with a dilemma, I solved the riddle. I decided every day would be adventure and excitement. Any disaster or consequence would become an opportunity to learn from what life decided to show me.

And once I made up my mind on this, the four-year reign of terror in my life otherwise known as writer's block finally lifted and allowed me passage.

Joy followed as I loosened the throttle and performed layout on multiple works, including *I Disappear: 3 Short Screenplays*, the second edition of *The Cadis Evening*, and now *Arusha: Poems & Essays*. With the release of *I Disappear*, I knew it was time to republish certain works that I'd previously suppressed. I planted many seeds years ago, and now it was time to take up that which had been planted- the gathering of the harvest... after I secured permissions, of course.

Poetry is art done with words. Someone said this. Maybe me? Or perhaps this is a truth that should be more universally known.

Poetry allows the writer to explore the random spaces, the undefinable, the higher and lower planes of thought. The power and magic of poetry is that the words are more than the sum of their parts. It is possible to say so much with so little because the reader of the poetry is allowed to interact with the words and interpret the meanings to their own lives and realities.

Poetry remains a tried and true method of exploring and then revealing the wide spectrum of life that ranges from pure beauty to pure horror. Is what I wrote just now making any sense? Yes? No? Maybe? If not, then I have just demonstrated the purpose poetry serves.

Poetry frees the writer to reveal the unspeakable, the inexpressible, the undefinable.

"On Street K [*Imaginarium*, 2006], "Dreams" [*Celara Sun*, 2010], "Silk and Silver" [*Sudan: The Lion of Truth*, 2nd ed, 2011], "Breakaway" [*Windrunner*, 2012], "Reverie" [*Road Romance: Tales from the Book Tour*], "The Ship of Fools" [*The Dark Fantastic: 12 Short Screenplays*, 2013], "Dreams in Arkana" [*The Cadis Evening*, 2016], "My Sweet Baby" [*Tamerlane* (unpublished), 2019], "The Mountains Reach" [*Disappear: 3 Short Screenplays*, 2020] are poems previously written that I hid in the very last pages of certain of my book-length works. And now, they are revealed.

"The Lion Roars" and "The Sun Shines" and "The People Live" are new poems from 2020 that I wrote with joy and relief and a sense of freedom upon my good-time behavior release from writer's block. "Damaged, But We Still Love You" is the very latest work from 2021 concerning complicated conversations regarding survival.

Essays provide a method to personalize non-fiction as a narrative expression of factual information or provide a point-of-view. Narrative non-fiction, some call this genre, or "holding forth." The following works serve as a personal viewpoint of the facts that life presented to me at that time.

"Tionne's Thoughts: Messages of Love and Hope for Lost Black Girlhood," (1999) I wrote as a journal submission. The essay, one of my earliest, was rejected. I dusted myself off and tried again [Aaliyah] and it was rejected again and then some more. Twenty-one years later I remembered that I was now a publisher myself. Here it is! Certain sections of the essay have been redacted out of consideration for others.

"The FTAA, Globalization & Race" (2001) dates back to the era of The Battle of Seattle, Y2K fear-mongering, and the Bush/Gore campaign. North America saw the rise of the technocrats with their goal of market and government domination via free trade and globalization. Techno-facism continued the unrestricted, unregulated capitalism that has only one ending... death.

"Wartime Dissent: A Black American tradition vindicated by history," (2002) was originally published in the *Touchstone* news journal that circulated in one of the most conservative regions of the United States, College Station, Texas. It was written as a detailed protest against the Iraq and Afghanistan Wars triggered by 9/11 and false evidence of "weapons of mass destruction."

"*Kindred* and *Beloved*: Dark fantasies of horrific history," (2006) was my entry essay for the Creative Writing Program at Northwestern University. Sadly, I was not accepted. I'm not sure why, but I certainly hope this essay wasn't the reason. I challenged myself to provide a fair and balanced perspective between two famous authors, but in my heart, I'm team Octavia Butler all the way. To this day I feel blessed that I was able to meet Butler, attend two of her book events in Chicago, and pick up an autograph or several.

"When We Were Greens" (2010) dates back to an earlier incarnation of the McQueen Press Official website where I posted this essay after multiple rejections of my multiple submissions to multiple publications. I followed this essay with a video by the same title, recorded and released 2010, posted to YouTube 2011. Both versions are filled with hope and optimism of the possibilities that the common man and woman can achieve despite chaos and turmoil contrasted with indifference and apathy at the top levels of society and government. And maybe... we will once more be green in Africa.

"Writing Influences" (2016) is a transcript of me on video discussing who I read and use as models for my own writing and why. Video released to YouTube 2016.

"Viewpoints" (2018) is a report of my official positions. A political science major, which I was and I guess still am, usually has opinions on a vast amount of political subjects and can be relied upon to eagerly hold forth at length on any number of these subjects, asked or not asked. I am nothing, if not reliable (and consistent) when it comes to having a point-of-view.

"Journey to Arusha" (2020) describes my escape from Babylon and how I used every bit of common sense and street smartness provided to me to negotiate the bureaucratic barriers that might have affected my future in ways I could never predict. A few others traveled before, during, and many after my journey and we have shared our stories. Together, we form the African Diaspora, a new tribe with growing membership in every nation on the Continent.

"My Personal Experience as a Teacher," (2020) is the summative essay I wrote to receive certification as a Teacher of English for Speakers of Other Languages. Even with my journey across the ocean, I did not stop writing, researching, or learning. Upon arrival, when I wasn't studying for TESOL certification, I was writing and publishing, learning Kiswahili, and creating curricula to teach the English classes I held several times per week.

"Riding the Piki Piki," (2020) defines the cultural disconnect I experienced upon arrival to Tanzania. While I'd journeyed through Mexico many times, Africa was completely new to me. And I had so much to learn. Letting go of pride and acknowledging mistakes in order to build a bridge to understand my new home was the first step. Reaching out, asking questions, and learning Kiswahili from the children to whom I taught English took down many barriers.

All the recent work notwithstanding, many of the older works I created from whispers on-campus, rumors online, and so-called conspiracy theories have now manifested as reality. Violations of the human body itself by the State are up for debate in various government bodies with the overt approval and encouragement of mainstream media and technocratic economic elites.

Contact, track, trace, quarantine, isolation, mandatory mask-wearing, and forced vaccination have arrived. Slavery of the body and perhaps the mind would be for the entire world not just certain population segments, according to the over-eager techno-fascist salesmen who are finally seeing their dreams of 2000 manifest in the real world of 2020.

The body horror of mutilation, mutation, and violation has inspired even more vacations from Western nations, not as tourists, but as political refugees. And many people now realize that the borders around the United States can also prevent citizens from leaving, not just illegal aliens from entering.

And people wonder, where is Harriet Tubman now? Who will free us? Where will we go? What shall we do?

Marcus Garvey, "Liberate the minds of men and ultimately you will liberate the bodies of men."

George Clinton, "Free your mind and your ass will follow."

Bob Marley, "Emancipate yourselves from mental slavery. None but ourselves can free our minds."

Liberate your mind.

Emancipate your mind.

Free your mind.

Always the first step.

Lee McQueen
January 2021

Tionne's *Thoughts*: Messages of Love and Hope for Lost Black Girlhood

[unpublished journal submission, 1999]

I attended the book signing for Tionne "T-Boz" Watkins's *Thoughts* in Buffalo, New York, November 1999. I purchased the book to reflect on the themes of beauty and sexuality, violence and oppression, and race and identity from the viewpoint of a young, contemporary African-American female with whom I strongly identify. Tionne is nearly the same age as me, just a few months apart. In this way, we are both part of that intriguing group of people called Generation X (those persons with the distinction of being born from 1965-1985.

Even though members of Generation X, including myself, actively reject the negative stereotypes of being slackers and apathetic towards the future, some of the stereotypes do describe my reality. As a result of reading *Thoughts*, I felt the courage to share my thoughts and emotions about my own reality as a young African-American female. My observations at the book signing, reflections of my life [redacted], and a personal reaction to *Thoughts* are included in this essay. I refer to "T-Boz" as Tionne in this essay to separate her identity as an author of essays and poetry from her identity as a songwriter. I use the terms Black and African-American interchangeably because I refer to myself as either Black or African-American.

I recognize Dolly, Tionne's manager, from the photos included in the book. She notices me writing, and we strike up a conversation. I show her the email requesting submissions for this anthology. I explain to her the reasons why I chose to discuss *Thoughts*. I inform her that I also grew up in Des

Moines and that my grandmother and her grandmother lived very close to one another. Dolly says she will ask Tionne to say hello to me.

Television cameras and crew arrive. The crowd is swelling and becoming restless. Fans are entertaining themselves by singing the TLC song, "Creep" and giggling. I have been at my bench for over an hour talking with the mother of a TLC fan.

The bench is my territory now. When I pull out a pen and a pad of paper to take notes on the action, everyone assumes that I am a reporter. I play along by being very quiet and thoughtful with a look of relaxed calm. I am starting to feel excited by it all too, but I don't want to be shuffled away as an out-of-control fan. By this time, the crowd is chanting "T-Boz," led by a little boy about nine or ten-years-old. I am afraid he will pass out soon because he is highly excited and his little face is turning red. Tionne is running a little late because she is doing an interview for the local television news station.

Finally, the crowd begins screeching because Tionne has arrived. Immediately, I notice that she is very beautiful and walks with her head high. She is poised in dealing with her fans and the television news crew. How does a Black woman acquire that kind of self-confidence and sense of calm? It is almost always the hard way. *Thoughts* describes Tionne's journey through life.

Tionne handles cries for her attention from several directions at the same time. Because of the sheer number of people who continue to arrive to wish Tionne well, I remain at my vantage point observing the crowd. The audio version of *Thoughts* plays in the background. I hope people are listening to her words. I hope the message is not lost to her status as a celebrity. In person, Tionne seems to understand her fans's feelings. They sense this and it creates a positive, albeit emotional vibe at the book signing.

The teenage girls are red-faced and crying and so are some of the boys. There are fans from various age and ethnic groups. TLC's music and Tionne's popularity cuts across race, ethnic, gender, age, and class lines. People know that she is accepting of lifestyles and appearances that are considered alternative from the mainstream [see "Confused," p. 13]. I did wonder about the more elderly people waiting in line. I assumed that most were parents of Tionne's fans. But some probably wandered into the bookstore as a weekly routine and decided to stick around because of the crowd.

In this way, her pleasant demeanor and positive message creates new fans. Some celebrities shy away from the moniker "role model" because of the pressure to behave in a positive way. Tionne seems to wear it with pride and honesty. For instance, while I'm hanging out at Media Play, I speak with an African-American fireman in the crowd. His thirteen-year-old daughter is in line with her girlfriends, waiting for an autograph. He is glad that Tionne came out and that her message is positive, especially with all the negative messages that come out of the music industry. He shares with me, "Nowadays, celebrity seems to be all about the dollar and people really don't care about anybody but themselves." Tionne addresses this issue in her poem, "Celebrities," p. 75, "Money is material and can't buy love. Fans don't worship, humans are not man above." Her essay, "TLC," p. 87 also touches on this issue.

I can see that the line is still extremely long. It's almost five o'clock and it's getting darker outside. I let Dolly know that I'm leaving. She quickly introduces me to Tionne's mother, Gayle Watkins. Her mother is beautiful. We play the "do you know this person or that person in Des Moines game" for a while. I tell her that I recently visited Des Moines to see my own mother who cares for my grandmother there. I tell her that the city has changed drastically from what I remembered as a child. The inner-city environment has become harder, harsher. While I lived elsewhere over the years, gang life took over in Iowa's larger cities. My younger female cousins deal with the consequences of that change in social environment daily and it breaks my heart.

Gayle's last words to me are, "Don't forget where you came from." I feel a sharp pang inside because I have forgotten. Perhaps my reading *Thoughts* and meeting with Tionne's mother was a signal to me to own up to the past, no matter how painful or disappointing.

I notice that positive and pleasant people, particularly, her mother and her manager surround Tionne. I'm reminded of one of those sayings from the old school. "You bring out what you're about." Tionne brings out positive response from her fans, friends, family, and colleagues. Pages 120-121 of *Thoughts* are filled with glowing praise from colleagues in the music industry such as Patti LaBelle, Paula Cole, and Jermaine Dupri.

Amazon.com quotes Kenneth "Babyface" Edmonds, "Poetry is still one of the purest and most intimate forms of creative expression. It is like a window to the soul... Tionne has in fact opened the window to her soul for the world to see." Amazon.com's own review states that the audio and tape formats of *Thoughts* "reveals yet again the breadth of Watkins's creativity and originality."

Publisher's Weekly (November 1, 1999) praises *Thoughts*, "The Iowa-born singer addresses issues that affect many teens: racism, health, weight, working—all components of self-image. Her message is one of self-reliance, born out in plainspoken rhyme..."

Most importantly, Tionne's fans love her work. They love *Thoughts*. They love her. This love extends from the fan reviews on Amazon.com, to the web-sites constructed in her honor, to the near hysteria of the book signing, to the parents who gaze with approval as she speaks gently and positively to young people.

I have always loved music and books. Poetry never moved me much in the early years though. It was difficult for me to understand. I needed the poet to make a point, to say exactly what they meant, and to skip the gibberish. Then I heard

Maya Angelou speak two years ago. Since then, I've begun to understand the power and magic of poetry, how the words are much more than the sum of their parts, how the reader is allowed to interact with poetry, how the ambiguity allows the reader to interpret the meaning of the words to their own lives and their own realities. Tionne's poetry speaks directly to the soul of the reader.

For those like me who have struggled to understand poetry in the past, struggle no more. Tionne's style is very clear. The essays and the poetry guides at the end of her book allow the reader to see straight into her heart. The affirmations remind me of Iyanla Vanzant's inspirational writings such as *Acts of Faith* or Maya Angelou's *Phenomenal Woman*. I also think of Susan Taylor's spiritual essays in *Essence Magazine*. The difference here is that Tionne is talking directly to the younger generation. However, I also recommend this book for anyone who seeks insight into the heart and mind of Black girlhood.

I enjoyed reading *Thoughts* even though I felt chilled in some parts as a suppressed memory or and unresolved issue rose to the surface. *Thoughts* creates accountability with the reader and lets the reader know, hey, I'm not perfect and you're not perfect, but we can still change what we don't like in ourselves. Even though you're not living the so-called American dream and you don't have what the media considers the all-American appearance, it doesn't mean that you are doomed to suffer unhappiness for the rest of your life. It doesn't make you a bad person. Is Tionne "T-Boz" Watkins the next Nikki Giovanni? I don't know. What I do know is that she is generous with the wisdom that she has accumulated up to this point.

She has paid that wisdom forward.

And for this reason alone, she has done well in life.

The FTAA, Globalization, and Race
[from The BlackElectorate.com, 2001]

FTAA is an expansion of NAFTA. NAFTA deregulated trade b/t Canada, the US, and Mexico. FTAA would deregulate trade from fvlaska down to Argentina with the sole exception being Cuba. In theory, free trade and the global village sound like a good warm and fuzzy "we are the world" idea. However, in practice, free trade benefits large corporations at the health and safety of workers of those corporations, not only in the US but in all 34 countries possibly involved.

Environmentalists, unions, prison activists, and students from around the world are demanding FAIR TRADE, not just free trade. Anti-globalization protest is no longer the US versus "them ferners." The issue is profit-motivated corporations verses poor and indigenous populations from around the world. Which is why anti-globalists in the US have united with anti-globalists in Mexico, Brazil, Europe, Africa, and on and on to fight against WTO, IMF, and GATT.

Anti-globalism is not a bored, rich, white liberal issue. The push for fair trade involves everyone affected by large corporate smothering - which is actually everyone. FTAA teach-ins, actions, demonstrations and protests are planned throughout the month of April with the most crucial days being April 19-22 during which world leaders in the Western hemisphere meet in Quebec City, Canada. Quebec City is currently a police state and many people will not be able to cross the border.

One alternative site for protest is Buffalo, NY and you can get more information here http://www.a22buffalo.org.

Protests are also planned in Cleveland, San Diego, and a few other border crossings. [See 90 events in 75 cities: http://www.a20.org/calendar.cfm]

For a clearer understanding of how FTAA will affect you, view this link http://stopftaa.org.

Particularly for people of color around the world, FTAA is relevant. Particularly for people in the United States of color and poor people, the anti-globalization movement is relevant to you if:

1   You are a white-collar worker (dot.com, telecommunications who was down-sized by a corporation during or after a merger despite your education and work skills. In an effort to make higher profits, one person works three times harder for the same pay and two people are fired.

2   You are a blue-collar worker (factory, construction) whose job was sent to Mexico or Bangladesh where corporate employers know they don't have to pay health insurance, a livable wage, or ensure worker safety, or worry about polluting the air and water. An underage child laborer now does what you do at one-fifth the cost. The child laborer is not the enemy. The corporation is.

3   You know people in jail and prison who do not belong there. Or maybe it was you who "fit the description" and did time. You were charged with a non-violent crime (such as passing bad checks, marijuana possession, loitering). Perhaps you were in the wrong place at the wrong time. You did time because you could not afford bail, did not have the right connections, and could not afford a good lawyer. Being beaten, raped, and degraded is not equal punishment for smoking a joint or bouncing a check.

A lucrative industry today is part of the prison-industrial complex. America's love of money has made us the world's largest jailer. Corrections Corporation of America, Wackenhut, prison construction firms, insurance agencies (Merrill Lynch), telecommunications (AT&T) and more need raw materials/product/commodities in order to increase profits. Rural towns whose main employment sources are now in Mexico and Bangladesh (as described in point 2) need jobs. If you are an ethnic minority, an immigrant, a political dissident, without connections, your body and life will become a source of income for the prison industry.

[http://www.theatlantic.com/issues/98dec/prisons.htm &
http://www.criticalresistance.org/mission.html]

If you consider it carefully, the prison-industrial complex has replaced slavery as a viable economic system for America. The similarities are frightening--mostly colored, poor, immigrants, and now women make up the largest growing prison population. Inside the system, these groups are beaten, raped, tortured, degraded, and controlled by rural whites who have no personal wealth and therefore welcome the chance to participate as guards. Prison inmate laborers are paid very little or sometimes not at all. Work + no pay = slavery. Women and men are used for sex and punished by other inmates and prison officials for resisting. All due to public officials turning a blind eye to the cries of protest (when they are not passing additional "tough-on-crime" legislation).

Largely colored prison populations are transported away from their families sometimes across state lines to fill beds in other communities. Remember, family separation was one way to weaken Blacks during slavery. Lani Guinier explained in the Black forum on C-SPAN that prisoners are counted in the Census as part of the rural white community. That rural white community receives federal funds that otherwise would go to the urban centers where the inmate lived before incarceration. And once released, after all the trauma, the ex-felon may be denied the right to vote although he may pay taxes. Ex-felons are counted, but not allowed to vote. Remember the famous 3/5ths of a person clause? See the parallels?

Slavery was the first American socio-economic effort to repress the Black voice. Segregation and Jim Crow was the second socio-economic effort to diminish Black power and self-determination. Today, the prison-industrial complex is the third act to place the voice of young, vital Black men and women under lock and key. Is it time for another Harriet Tubman, Frederick Douglass, Nat Turner to speak and act out on a system that while legal is at the same time brutal, barbaric, and morally unjust? I think so.

4   If your neighborhood smells to high heaven. If the air you breathe is brown. If the women in your family find tumors and cancerous growths more frequently in strange places. If the men in your family experience high rates of prostate cancer not due to diet or smoking. If your child plays in areas where lead paint is still lying on the ground and peeling off the walls. If you have begun purchasing distilled water because the tap water is no longer drinkable. If parks are giving way to parking lots. Then the anti-environmental realities of FTAA would definitely concern you.

5   Speaking of children, if your child is profiled at school as a behavior problem, low-intelligence, and maybe having a short-attention span...the school may prescribe Ritalin, Prozac, or other drugs to regulate his behavior. If you refuse the drugging of your child, you may be held liable. The pharmaceutical companies are amazing lobbyists and it would not be difficult to give a private (or public) school this type of legal power over your child. Currently, Rod Paige, the Secretary of Education has allowed the practice of Channel One, whereby corporations are allowed to advertise their products in the classroom by paying off the school district. If your child suddenly develops a thirst for Coca-Cola, you'll know why.

6   If you are alarmed at what is happening to the world food supply in regards to Mad Cow disease, Hoof and Mouth disease, and genetically-modified corn (not approved by the FDA) finding its way into a supermarket near you, the free trade trend of privatizing social policies such as food regulation with an eye to profit would definitely concern you.

7   Again, NAFTA and FTAA trade deregulation do not equal "free" trade. There is nothing free about it. To have an idea of how deregulation can affect your life directly, those folks in California can review their latest electric bills and decide how unfree free trade and deregulation actually can be. Imagine what free trade can do for the price of your electricity, natural gas, and gasoline.

8   If you know of someone or you, yourself are affected by AIDS, FTAA has the possibility of keeping the price of drug treatments out of your range unless you can afford $15,000-20,000/yr for effective treatment. Currently Brazil, India, South Africa, and Cuba are refusing to buy drugs manufactured by prescription corporations because corporate prices are inflated beyond belief. Instead, these countries are basically saying "f--- you" to the pharmaceutical corporations and are manufacturing generic drugs that cost $1/day or $365/yr. Brazil said screw it and are now giving away the AIDS drugs for free. If the US has its way, it will put increased regulations in the FTAA to prevent the production of cheap but effective generic AIDS drugs. Anyone with HIV and AIDS who does not have $15,000-20,000/yr to spend will die in the name of profit. These drugs were developed using public tax money and now the finished product is being withheld in the name of profit.

[Read about it here http://www.a2o.org/feature.cfm?ID=45]

9   We've already seen how large corporations affect the entertainment industry. Radio, television, and film are controlled by approximately five corporations now. These corporations control content, access, and visibility. If these corporations feel their profits will be threatened by the content or visibility of independent voices, it is easy to pull the plug and join other corporations to quash and blacklist the activists.

The latest episode with Tavis Smiley, BET, and Viacom is but one example in television. Viacom has won approval from Michael Powell's FCC to purchase UPN. With BET and UPN safely under its authority, Viacom has vast control over what little Black expression remains on television.

Other examples are the payoffs that result in radio airplay given to low-quality music in all genres. Also in radio, independent stations, such as Pacifica are being forcibly shut down. Spike Lee's *Bamboozled* reveals how Black expression in film and television are corporate-controlled to the point

Scary Movie will make millions due to heavy promotion, but quality independent Black films like *The Visit* are ignored.

Lucky for us we have the Internet. For now. Michael Powell, Colin Powell's son is head of the FCC. Both Powells have never met a merger they did not like. With AOL and Microsoft negotiating for ever-increasing control of information technology, we may have to go back to beating drums in order to have free and open communication systems.

10 Okay, now I'm going to get really wacky with you. I've discussed healthcare, telecommunications, and criminal justice. Where do these different social policies meet? In a new technology being developed called Digital Angel. [See http://www.digitalangel.net/da/uses.htm].

DA is currently being marketed as a means to track lost children, seniors, and pets. But it is also being billed as a multi-million dollar industry which makes it highly unlikely that Digital Angel will be limited to children, seniors, and lost pets or even livestock. A multi-million dollar industry needs more people than that. The technology is also a possibility to track military personnel, prisoners, and people who have "bad thoughts."

The manufacturer, Applied Digital Solutions, is quietly partnering with medical manufacturers right now. After FTAA, the sky would be the only limit for a multi-million dollar industry whose main goal is to track and monitor people and objects. How many campaign donations would it take before Digital Angel is legislated as a required for every child attending public school, any student wishing to enroll in college, all military, anyone who's ever entered the criminal justice system, anyone who receives a vaccination (DA is as small as a grain of rice) and can be worn as a watch-like device or injected under the skin.

Digital Angel is currently voluntary. But, once upon a time, vaccinations and Social Security numbers were voluntary. While it is probably possible to get through life without a smallpox vaccine or SS#, it is not easy. I'm speculating here, but you look at the site and judge for yourself how endless the possibilities are for required monitoring devices. Unless you don't mind a centralized corporate-controlled agency knowing where you are at all times. Will those of us with the misfortune to reside in the prison-industrial complex find ourselves "Running Men," much like Arnold Schwartzenegger's character in that movie? With the possibility of a televised, or even bootleg digitized execution forthcoming with Timothy McVeigh, plus the rise of semi-reality television programming, it remains a possibility.

I will end the speculation here.

I hope I've made the possibility of what FREE versus FAIR trade can bring and how what happens in Quebec City during April 19-22 will change lives. The problems that are visible right now, will be magnified but only if mainstream media reports it. We may all be told by the five largest media corporations to take Prozac, listen to a Britney Spears CD, or watch a Jim Carrey movie and get over it.

It doesn't have to be that way if the people whose lives are affected speak up now. If you read through this long post and have felt the affects of corporate domination over your jobs, your civil rights, your healthcare, your access mainstream media and telecommunications, your employment and unemployment, your environment, your food quality, and your childcare, NOW is the time to speak up BEFORE FTAA is ratified and given final approval.

Go to http://www.stopFTAA.org and read about it and decide for yourself where you fit in.

You'll have to seek information about FTAA on your own because mainstream coverage will focus on how "fringe groups" are breaking glass windows for no reason. I've outlined ten reasons for protest. But there are many more.

War Time Dissent: A Black American Tradition Vindicated by History

[from *The Touchstone*, Vol. XII, No. 1, Feb./Mar. 2002]

Huge demonstrations of black protest greeted the Italian invasion of Ethiopia in 1935. Stokely Carmichael's and Martin Luther King Jr.'s public condemnation of the Vietnam War -- against the 'better judgment' of many liberals (Black and white alike) -- was a watershed in the 1960s. The wave of mass opposition to the Reagan-Bush administration's support of South Africa's apartheid regime is likely the most well known example. And more recently, we should not forget that the Congressional Black Caucus stood mostly alone in Congress in protest of the U.S. overthrow of the democratically elected government of Grenada." -- Frances M. Beal, Black America and the Struggle for Peace, *Michigan Citizen*, October 21, 2001.

The attacks of September 11th, the release of the Ali movie, the celebration of Martin Luther King's birthday, and the advent of Black History Month otherwise known as February have converged to fill me with a sense of urgency in drawing together the threads of time that link Black American presence in America from slavery to the present as voices of dissent and concern for America's morality. When reading coverage of the "traitors, cowards, and terrorist sympathizers" who happen to be Black, lurking among the "true patriots" who happen to be White, it causes me to raise the question ... How on Earth Did We Ever Get Here? How did criticism and caution come to equal treason and sympathy for terrorism?

Rather than going on at length on how I feel about the racial epithets that accompany the typical "If you hate America so much then go back where you came from" recommendation, and rather than make repeated attempts to justify dissent as a cornerstone of democracy, I wish to allow history and the passage of time to do that by providing an extensive list of quotes from historical Black dissenters whose words and deeds garnered hatred and anger from the moderate-to-conservative mainstream of both Black and White cultures at the time.

Frederick Douglass was the most effective and imposing Black speaker and author of his time, he being a former slave, abolitionist, editor, orator, reformer, and champion of human rights. Doubtless, Black men and women held opinions of America's war policies prior to Frederick Douglass, particularly since Black men had fought on behalf of America in both the war of Independence in 1776 and again in 1812. But written records of Black opinion and thought are understandably scarce since reading and writing by Blacks was against the law and most Whites were not interested in how they felt about the wars of that time.

From Frances Beal's commentary on Black America and the Struggle for Peace published in the *Michigan Citizen*, October 21, 2001 we know that "As far back as 1848, for example, Frederick Douglass condemned U.S. aggression against Mexico as disgraceful, cruel and iniquitous. His son Lewis spoke out 51 years later to deplore U.S. policy in regard to Cuba, the Philippines, Hawaii and Puerto Rico as hypocrisy of the most sickening kind."

In his speech "What to the Slave is the Fourth of July?" delivered on July 4, 1852, and published in My Bondage and My Freedom, Frederick Douglass also commented on the celebration of America's War of Independence from Great Britain by saying, "What to the American slave is your Fourth of July? I answer, a day that reveals to him, more than all other days in the year, the gross injustices and cruelty to which he is the constant victim ... Go where you may, search where you will, roam through all the monarchies and despotisms of the old world, travel through South America, search out every abuse, and when you have found the last, lay bare your facts by the side of the every-day practices of this nation, and you will say with me, that for revolting barbarity, and shameless hypocrisy, America reigns without a rival." And in so doing, Douglass laid the foundation for the worthy and honorable tradition of protesting America's efforts for imperialism and colonialism and suppression of people of color as a foreign and domestic policy to uphold White supremacy.

Black press, in general, followed the tradition of Douglass's editorship by using the written word as a tool to voice their opinions on the marginal status of the Black in America. For instance, a Baltimore Afro-American editorial written in December 29, 1929 makes the statement regarding the dispatch of Marines to Haiti during bludgeoning and lynching of blacks in Sherman, Texas: "If the marines must fight, we suggest that President Hoover order them to Mississippi, Alabama, Texas and Georgia."

Further, Richard Wright, prior to the Pearl Harbor attack that marked the entry of the United States into World War 2 delivered a speech, "Not My People's War", on June 6, 1941 before the League of American Writers council meeting. He basically stated that WW2 was not a war black people should participate in because of their treatment in America. However, in a show of solidarity and in an effort to "close ranks" to score the "double-v" of victory (equality) at home and conquest abroad for Black enlistees, Wright modifies his tone on December 15, 1941 by stating, "I pledge my loyalty and allegiance, without mental reservation or evasions, to America. I shall through my writing seek to rally the Negro people to stand shoulder to shoulder with the Administration in a solid national front to wage war until victory is won." (Michael Fabre, *The Unfinished Quest of Richard Wright*, University of Illinois, 1993).

Like Frederick Douglass during the Civil War and W.E.B. Dubois during World War 1, Wright held the optimistic view that if Blacks proved their loyalty to the United States government by fighting for freedom abroad, they would reap the reward of freedom at home. In the later Cold War years, W.E.B. Dubois made a joint statement with actor/activist Paul Robeson and Benjamin Davis, et al, "We Charge Genocide" in New York in 1951. "White supremacy at home makes for colored massacres abroad ... lyncher and the atom bomber are related." And so, Dubois recognized that silent, quiet loyalty breeds the perception of acquiescence to the unacceptable status quo of second-class citizenship of Black Americans.

A *Crisis* editorial LVIII written in the August-September edition in 1950 outlines the recognition by Black Americans that their treatment within U.S. borders mirrored the treatment of people of color abroad by the U.S. The hypocrisy and irony of America's stance for freedom was impossible to ignore: "... We will never win the political war in Asia as long as Koreans and Asiatics are gooks in the eyes of our fighting men. Whether we know it or not, Asia is in revolution. Her people fight for nationhood. Here is America's opportunity to live up to her own revolutionary past by helping the struggling masses of Asia to economic security and political independence."

Paul Robeson stepped up to the plate to confront America's march towards imperialism and made it relevant for Black Americans in his autobiographical book Here I Stand, "... if we don't stop our armed adventure in Korea today tomorrow it will be Africa." And earned the full wrath, hatred, and anti-communist hysteria that laid in wait for Blacks who protested the United States government for any reason whether it be lynching, brutality, discrimination, etc.

Robeson continues, "When will Americans learn, that if they would encourage liberty in other countries, they must practice it at home? ... The world has learned the terrible lesson of Hitler: racism, backed by the power and technology of a modern industrial state, is a monster that must never be unleashed again. What difference is there between the Master Race idea of Hitler and the White supremacy creed of Eastland? Who can convince the European peoples that the burning cross of the white-robed Klan is different from the swastika of the Brownshirts? America, of course, is not a fascist nation, but the deep-rooted racism here and its violent outbursts arouse the worst fears of those who survived the holocaust of Hitlerism."

From the *Autobiography of W.E.B. Dubois*, Robeson's treatment as a direct result of his dissent is assessed thusly by Dubois: "The persecution of Paul Robeson by the government ... has been one of the most contemptible happenings in modern history." Thus, we learn that it was not only writers and scholars who practiced dissent as an American tradition. Artists and entertainers with the benefit of worldly experience on foreign stages were able to assess their domestic situations with a broad view.

Josephine Baker spoke to *Critica* on October 6, 1952 and said the following in regards to World War 2: "I met thousands of Americans from the North and from the South. They believed, in good faith, that they were fighting for democracy and civilization that were being menaced by totalitarianism. Many had no hesitation in expressing their horror and their indignation at the news of massacres of Jewish prisoners. But as for the Negro, the Southerners still continued and now keep on thinking that all the evil that is done is all right, and is necessary. How they reconciled these two opinions is something I have still not been able to figure out."

She continues her insightful observations by saying, "Unless there is a halt to the wave of lynchings, electrocutions without proof, collective aggressions and other beauties of the American way of life, it means that all the blood spilled in the last war has been in vain. The apparent enemies of Hitler see his triumph multiplied in the Southern United States." Like Robeson, Baker caught the attention of the U.S. government enraged by her audacity in speaking with foreign press about "family issues."

However, the efforts to censor and red-bait and ruin did not stop Louis Armstrong in the Fall of 1957 from remarking, "The way they are treating my people in the South, the government can go to hell ... The people over there [Soviet Union] ask me what's wrong with my country, what am I supposed to say? ... The Government could go to the devil with its plans for a propaganda tour of Soviet Russia."

Malcolm X, the ultimate Black radical is quoted in Clyde Taylor's *Vietnam and Black America* as saying, "If it is right for America to draft us, and teach us how to be violent in defense of her, then it is right for you and me to do whatever is necessary to defend our own people right here in this country." Malcolm X was assassinated in 1965.

Risking the benevolence of White liberals and alienating many Black supporters, Martin Luther King Jr., acknowledged his internal disturbance regarding the Vietnam War in several sermons. In "Strength to Love" delivered in New York in 1964, he said: "We must not engage in a negative anti-Communism, but rather in a positive thrust for democracy ... we must with positive action seek to remove those conditions of poverty, insecurity, injustice, and racial discrimination which are the fertile soil in which the seed of Communism grows ... Millions of citizens are deeply disturbed that the military-industrial complex too often shapes national policy, but they do not want to be considered unpatriotic. Countless loyal Americans honestly feel that a world body such as the United Nations should include Red China, but they fear being called Communist sympathizers. A legion of thoughtful persons recognizes that traditional capitalism must continually undergo change if our great national wealth is to be more equitably distributed, but they are afraid their criticisms will make them seem un-American."

His words are profound and prophetic because King WAS considered un-American and a communist sympathizer because of his views on civil rights and peace. Martin Luther King gave a speech at fundraiser for the *Nation* magazine on February 25, 1967: "We are engaged in a war that seeks to turn the clock of history back and perpetuate white colonialism. The bombs in Viet Nam explode at home and they destroy the hopes and possibilities for a decent America ... We must combine the fervor of the civil rights movement with the peace movement. We must demonstrate, teach and preach, until the very foundations of our nation are shaken."

Finally, Martin Luther King Jr. joined Stokely Carmichael at a United Nations rally in 1967 fully protesting and dissenting the draft of Black men for the Vietnam War: "Hell no, we wont go!" Black wartime dissent boiled over in 1967. Martin Luther King Jr. even commented on rising Republican political hawk and future Cold Warrior, Ronald Reagan in *Domestic Impact of the War*: "... a Hollywood performer, lacking distinction even as an actor..."

The ever-loquacious Muhammad Ali declared, "I ain't got nothing against them Viet Congs. No, I'm not going ten thousand miles from here to help murder and kill and burn another poor people simply to help continue the domination of white slavemasters over the darker people the world over." Moreover, "I ain't got no quarrel with them Viet Cong." (G. Marine, Nobody Knows My Name, *Ramparts*, 5:12, June, 1967). And finally, the famous exclamation, "No Viet Cong never called me nigger!" the quote that Ali borrowed from Stokely Carmichael. Ali was rewarded for his defiance with attacks by mainstream press, a jail term, the stripping of his heavyweight championship title, and a distancing of the Black mainstream that supported the U.S. foreign policy.

Martin Luther King Jr. continued to voice dissent of the Vietnam War with his speech, "Where Do We Go From Here?" delivered in New York, 1968, losing the support of many followers, gaining the support of others: "These are revolutionary times. All over the globe men are revolting against old systems of exploitation and oppression, and out of a frail world new systems of justice and equality are being born. The shirtless and barefoot people of the earth are rising up as never before." King was assassinated later the same year.

Eldridge Cleaver, in a bid to reach moderate Blacks who absorbed war propaganda through choice or intimidation, warned, "Once the white man solves his problem in the East, he will turn his fury again on black people in America." (*Soul on Ice*, New York: McGraw-Hill, 1968).

The bitterness and anger of the rapid succession of assassinations [Malcolm X, JFK, MLK, RFK], the blood in the jungles of Vietnam and Cambodia, and the blood on the streets of urban America took its toll on American society as a whole. An unnamed Black Veteran speaks a widely felt sentiment of Black men in America, "The brothers thought that because they fought and saw their buddies die it would make a difference. But they came back to SOS-the same old stuff ... It's business as usual in America, and business as usual means black people are going to catch hell." (Thomas Johnson, "Negro Veteran is Confused and Bitter", *New York Times*, 29 July 1969).

As did entertainers Robeson, Baker, and Armstrong previously, artists used their unique gifts to express the pain and confusion of a world that no longer made sense. Marvin Gaye asked the million-dollar question: "What's goin' on?" and beautifully articulated the observations: "There's too many of you crying" and "There's far too many of you dying" and "We don't need to escalate" and "War is not the answer" and revealingly "Picket lines and picket signs, don't punish me with brutality." (*What's Goin' On?* 1971).

In addition, Harry Belafonte, Dick Gregory, Diana Ross, Jimi Hendrix denounced the war while keeping their audiences intact. By that time, dissent was no longer a unique experience among Black Americans. Charles B. Howell, a retired black veteran of 22 years of service stated that, "I think I'd shoot one of my kids before I let them fight for this country." (Richard Strayer and Lewis Ellenhorn, "Vietnam Veterans: A Case Study Exploring Adjustment Patterns and Attitudes", *Journal of Social Issues*, 31:4, 1975).

Fast-forward to the events of September 11, 2001. An unbelievable, unthinkable, unimaginable, horrible tragedy gripped the American psyche and held it hostage to visual imagery of towering, burning infernos sparked by terrorism. The calls for revenge, retaliation, and blinding eye-for-an-eye jingoism began immediately.

Congresswoman Barbara Lee (D-CA) rose before the House of Representatives to explain her lone vote against use-of-force resolution on September 14, 2001. "There must be some of us who say, lets step back for a moment and think through the implications of our actions today. Let us more fully understand their consequences. As we act, let us not become the evil that we deplore."

"With Liberty at Risk," written on September 19, 2001, John Conyers (D-MI) who represents a large Arab population, warned: "Historically, it has been at times of inflamed passions and national anger that our civil liberties proved to be at greatest risk, and the unpopular group of the moment was subject to prejudice and deprivation of liberty. In 1798, Congress enacted the notorious Alien and Sedition Acts, making it a federal crime to criticize the government. In 1861, at the beginning of the Civil War, President Lincoln suspended habeas corpus, citing the need to repress 'an insurrection against the laws of the United States.' Ulysses S. Grant sought to expel Jews from southern states. World War II brought about the shameful internment of Japanese Americans, which even the Supreme Court failed to overturn."

The voice of caution and concern rose again with Michael Eric Dyson's appearance on *Politically Incorrect*, September 24, 2001. From the transcript, his views require no additional context. "... in Tulsa, Oklahoma, an all-Black community was established historically established. They had their own banks, their own systems of delivery of goods and services: highly educated Black people. And because of the resentment, the collective resentment of the white folk, who were there against the Black folk, they went out and looted their stores, burned their homes, and killed these people in massive numbers. And I'm saying, what's interesting to me is that, now that I see America hurtling toward war, I ask, should Black people have responded against their white brothers and sisters in the same way that we now want to respond to our brothers and sisters throughout the world? I don't romanticize bin Laden, because he started in Africa [allegedly bombed the U.S. embassy in the Sudan]. Let's not get it twisted. He doesn't have solidarity with people of color. The reality however, is that African-American people in particular, but others as well, understand that low-grade terrorism is what we confront in this nation every day. You tell me about arbitrary violence. What happens if you think my son who lives in Atlanta, will he go out today and, reaching for his wallet some policeman mistake it for a gun and then murder him? I tell you, that's terroristic to me. Now, it's low-grade, it's not on the spectacular scale about which you've spoke, but it is an insidious every day factor that robs us of a sense of security in this nation. And that's what I think we all feel. That's why I say were all Black now. Everybody understands what it means to be Black right now in America."

Aaron McGruder, author of *The Boondocks* comic strip [http://www.ucomics.com/boondocks] determined that there is more to the terrorist attacks than the American public is allowed to hear and on October 4, 2001, pens a cartoon that is pulled from major newspapers for mocking a former president and the investigation (or lack thereof) into the September 11 tragedy. "Huey calls the FBI's terrorism tip line ... I'm very serious. I know of several Americans who have helped train and finance Osama bin Laden ... The first one is Reagan. That's R-E-A-G ... Hello? Hello?"

Congresswoman Cynthia McKinney's "Official Statement" of October 16, 2001 provided a caveat to her vote of support in Congress: "... When I voted for the War Powers Resolution, I did not surrender my right to express my views and opinions or to continue to advocate for justice and human rights in America or around the world. I believe that American security will be enhanced by a foreign policy that positions the United States as an honest broker for justice in the Middle East."

Danny Glover's speech at an anti-death penalty forum at Princeton University on November 16, 2001 inflamed right-wing vituperation and calls for a boycott and blacklist chillingly reminiscent of Paul Robeson's treatment during the Cold War almost fifty years earlier. Glover stated, "This week, President Bush implemented a military tribunal which will make it easier for us to execute (people). This clearly is a slippery slope. We must stand vigilant against Bush in these times ... We shouldn't let the federal government destroy individual rights."

The sharp dissent continued with Boots Riley of the rap group, The Coup, whose album cover strangely foretold the events of September 11th before it was pulled prior to distribution. "There are mainstream artists I know who are against the war but think they'll be blacklisted if they come out officially against it. They don't want to get involved. The silence is huge. People are scared. They're so used to media making it seem like no one is dissenting in this war that they're afraid to voice their opinion ... I want to fight the McCarthyist state that's developing in this country so my kids won't live in a world where people are afraid to speak out. I've always done that, but I have to work even harder now." (*The San Francisco Chronicle*, November 18, 2001).

More of Generation X continued to make their views public when Kevin Powell shared dialogue on January 23, 2002 with *Davey D's Hip Hop Corner* on the Internet at http://www.daveyd.com/FullArticles/articleN958.asp. "... I thought about Black people, a lot, Charlie. Black people are not new to tragedy, as you well know. As Langston Hughes once said eloquently in a poem, I've known rivers. Collectively, we've known rivers. So I saw this tragedy with a different set of eyes, so to speak. I saw it with the eyes of a people who had been ripped from their native land, Africa, stripped of themselves, their language, their spirits, their minds, made to hate themselves, and made into slaves. That, too, is a form of terrorism to me.

"I saw it with the eyes of a people who had been told they were free, after slavery, only to endure another 100 years of second-class citizenship, only to endure lynchings, cheap or underpaid labor, the stealing of whatever land some of them might have had (as had happened to my great-grandfather in South Carolina), denial of the right to vote, denial of the right to be a citizen and, really, denial of the right to be human beings.

I saw it with the eyes of a people who, in spite of the great Civil Rights Movement, still had to live in the ghettoes of America, the majority of us, anyhow, dealing with poor communities, poor schools, poor resources, just a vicious cycle of poverty and madness. And I saw it with the eyes of folks in our communities who have and do experience their own form of terrorism, what I think Michael Eric Dyson called slow terrorism because of what things like AIDS and crack and police brutality have done to us, and does to us everyday ... When I think about all the reactions that have come since September 11th, the detaining of Arab Americans in this country, the plans to deport thousands of Arab Americans who are suspected of criminal activity, the deep anti-Muslim sentiments, the zealousness with which many people in and outside of the government have called for war and revenge, the calls for United We Stand, the waving of American flags and the wearing of flag tee shirts, hats, pins, and other items, I can't help but wonder how wounded America was as a country before September 11th if we could be so instantly reactionary after the tragedy. In other words, given the magnitude of what happened, does it not make sense for us to assess everything? History, American foreign policy, this country's on-going problem of dealing with its own racism toward people of color, the propensity of this country to solve everything by violent means ..."

Frances M. Beal clarifies the history of Black dissent further with the article, "Black America and the Struggle for Peace" (October 2001). "Our distinct history as a specially oppressed people -- as property, as cannon fodder, as second-class citizens, as targets of state terror in the form of police violence -- is the taproot of identification with the oppressed throughout the world. No amount of patriotism can hide another ugly truth. The burden of war takes a tremendous -- and disproportionate -- toll on the Black community. According to official Department of Defense statistics regarding Vietnam, "Blacks were more likely to be (1) drafted (30% to 19%); (2) sent to Vietnam; (3) serve in high risk combat units; and consequently, (4) to be killed or wounded in battle." In fact, between 1961 and 1966 Black casualties topped 20% of total combat fatalities -- when Black youth aged 19-21 constituted only 11% of military personnel in Vietnam. Today, it is estimated that Blacks constitute 25% of the military, and in ground troop personnel, estimates range as high as 35-40%."

No wonder Black people choose to dissent when their very lives are at stake!

Rap group, Public Enemy, declared the same eleven years prior in the song, "Bring the Noise" from *It Takes a Nation of Millions to Hold Us Back* (1988). "They'll never care for the brothers and sisters now across the country has us up for a war."

And my conclusion as it relates to the backlash against those Blacks who chose to speak out in wake of the terrorist attacks this past September is as follows: History has vindicated the Black radical, the subversive, the so-called "traitors" and "un-American evildoers," and all other "ungrateful" Black Americans who stood against the mainstream and chose to voice their dissent of policies they deemed as truly un-American and destructive to the lives of American citizens each and every single time. From Slavery and Jim Crow, to the Cold Wars in Korea and Vietnam, Black dissent and protest of America's over-expansion of power against poor people of color foreign and domestic has been vindicated by the passage of time as legitimate criticism protected by the First Amendment and historically, the moral and right choice.

The hated and the hunted, the surveilled and the jailed are revered as American icons today Frederick Douglass, Martin Luther King, Muhammad Ali, Fannie Lou Hamer, Sojourner Truth, Ida B. Wells, etc. What is unfortunate is that their vindication arrived decades after their deaths or during their slow decline to old age. The apologies and admissions of mistaken judgment allow those who actively sought to destroy their lives to ease the pain of a guilty conscience and mistakes in judgment.

Which leads me to wonder how long will it take for Congresswoman Barbara Lee, actor Danny Glover, and others who put their careers, their reputations and their very lives in danger by cautioning against rash military action in vengeful response to terrorist actions on September 11th? How long will it take before even moderate Black, White, Yellow, Red, and Brown Americans who currently support the U.S. governments hawkish foreign policy begin to understand how past declared and especially undeclared wars turned on the poor and ethnic groups in America as scapegoats? From the Cold War which red-baited and race-baited civil rights activists as communist sympathizers to the Drug War which baited people of color, particularly inner-city dwellers as criminal predators, soft-on-crime, and criminal sympathizers to this current War on Terrorism which brands any dissenter, any Arab, any Muslim, as a terrorist traitor and/or sympathizer, it is possible to see a repetition of social control through fear and scapegoating of ethnic groups via "wartime" propaganda.

Dissent is not only an American tradition since slavery for Black Americans, it is a patriotic, constitutional duty for all Americans to show love for ones nation by ensuring the principles upon which it was founded remain in place for the next generation as explained by The Coups Boots Riley. To stand silently by while the Constitution is violated via a presidential election concluded by voter disenfranchisement, while unofficial war is declared by a president who bypassed Congress, while citizens and foreign nationals who share characteristics with the alleged terrorists are rounded up on "secret" evidence, while anti-terror legislation is implemented that violates civil liberties, and government "of, by, and for the people" withdraws into secrecy in the face of alarming changes to long-standing tenets of democracy .. is unpatriotic, anti-democratic, and un-American.

Repressive behavior such as this more resembles a police state and dictatorship rather than a democracy worthy of being called America. It is time to reflect and learn from America's violent past beginning with Native American genocide, the Spanish Inquisition in Mexico, the Salem Witch Hunts, Slavery, Jim Crow, Southern Lynching, McCarthyism and Red-baiting, COINTELPRO against civil rights groups, assassinations, and the Drug War all distinctly un-American, but, actually, so very American.

It may be that I, myself, will be asked to respond to the long-standing, famous question "If you hate America so much, why don't you go back to Africa?" My response would be similar in nature to that of Paul Robeson when the House Un-American Activities Committee questioned him in 1956. One of the congressional investigators asked why, if Robeson liked Russia so much, "... why did you not stay in Russia?" And Robeson responds, "Because my father was a slave, and my people died to build this country, and I'm going to stay right here and have a part of it, just like you. And no fascist-minded people like you will drive me from it. Is that clear?"

Black Muslim and Nation of Islam leader Minister Louis Farrakhan echoes Robeson's powerful words with this statement of September 22, 2001, broadcast via satellite and Internet "... I'm critical of the government in aspects of their behavior toward Black people. It doesn't mean I hate America. I'm critical. And because I have the freedom, because of that great constitutional guarantee, to speak even if people do not like what I say, it is the freedom to speak that guarantees America a greater future. When you stifle voices that may disagree with you, you're only stifling something that could cause you to reason beyond your own bias, your prejudice, or your own views..." Criticism does not equal hate. Criticism equals a desire to see a better world and a full realization of potential.

I am an American. This is my country. It is my home. I refuse to sit idly and silently by while it is diminished by greed, fear, and hatred. History, as I've shown here, tells me and you that it is our patriotic, democratic, American duty to dissent against a government that has cut itself off from accountability and no longer exists "of, by, or for the people." To not dissent is unpatriotic and un-American.

Additional works cited:

Finkle, Lee. Forum for Protest: *The Black Press During World War II*. Madison: Associated University Presses, 1975.

Gilmore, Brian. "Stand By The Man: Black America and the Dilemma of Patriotism". *The Black World Today*, December 28, 2001.

Krenn, Michael L. (editor). *Race and U.S. Foreign Policy from the Colonial Period to the Present: A Collection of Essays*. New York: Garland Publishing, Inc, 1998.

Robeson, Paul. *Here I Stand*. Boston: Beacon Press, 1971.

Smith, Jessie Carney (editor). *Notable Black American Men*. Detroit: Gale, 1998.

Kindred and Beloved:
Dark fantasies of horrific history
[Admission Essay, Northwestern University 2006]

Two fictional explorations of North America's slavery past reveal the intense psychological and physical brutality inflicted on the free labor that pushed a fledgling nation to the forefront of the Industrial Revolution. Both *Kindred* (Octavia Butler, 1979) and *Beloved* (Toni Morrison, 1987) bridge the gap between romanticized fictional versions of the antebellum South such as *Uncle Tom's Cabin* (Harriet Beecher Stowe, 1852), *Huckleberry Finn* (Mark Twain, 1884), and *Gone with the Wind* (Margaret Mitchell, 1936) with grim but inspirational slave narratives such as *Incidents in the Life of a Slave Girl* (Harriet Jacobs, 1861), *The History of Mary Prince, a West Indian Slave* (Mary Prince, 1831), and *Narrative of the Life of Frederick Douglass, An American Slave* (Frederick Douglass, 1845).

Authors

Octavia Butler, born in 1947 in Pasadena, California, has been a freelance writer since 1970 winning numerous prestigious awards in the science fiction genre including one Hugo for "Speech Sounds" in 1984 and another for "Bloodchild" in 1985. She also won two Nebula Awards, one for "Bloodchild" in 1985 and *Parable of the Talents* in 1998. However, with the MacArthur Fellowship (also known as the "Genius Award") in 1995, Butler garnered even wider recognition for her body of work.

Born in 1931 in Lorain, Ohio, Toni Morrison worked within the publishing industry as book editor from 1965 to 1983. She taught English at several prestigious universities. In 1977, she won the National Book Critics Circle Award for Song of Solomon. She won the Pulitzer Prize for *Beloved* in 1988. In addition, she won the Nobel Prize for Literature in 1993. In 1996, Morrison won the National Book Foundation Medal for Distinguished Contribution to American Letters and the National Humanities Medal in 2001.

Both Butler and Morrison chose to write about peculiar times in nineteenth-century North America from the point-of-view of black females caught within the slave system, over one hundred years after the Thirteenth Amendment formally abolished slavery in the United States and its territories. Both Butler and Morrison explored the plight of black female slaves by coloring in the gaps between slave narratives that hid despair below dignity, news clippings that told only one side of the story, legal documents that reduced human tragedy to statistics, and romantic fictions that observed the degradation of human soul and spirit from the sidelines.

Styles

Morrison, well-known for her complex and layered storytelling technique applied a similar style to *Beloved*. The story of a woman haunted by the horrors of the past via a terror of the present swirls into a whirlpool of poetic depth in which the reader sometimes loses his or her way. Then, unexpectedly, the disjointed layers click sharply into place like a kaleidoscope. Her writing is raw and deals intensely with the train wreck of shameful history from which the reader would like to avert his or her eyes, but simply cannot. This is dramatic, literary fiction. In Morrison's writing, one central protagonist tends to share focus with a strong supporting cast, usually other women, who all experience a great amount of internal and external conflict.

In contrast, Butler's spare, linear, lean, stark and unflinchingly direct literary style slices away extraneous words to vividly reveal time and place as well as character motivation. She describes detailed social communities whether present day, near future, far future, or historical that chauffe[u]r the reader on a wondrous journey through science and fantasy. Like most of her other fiction, *Kindred* features a strong, central female protagonist who endures great trials, challenges traditional society and culture, and eventually emerges as a leader.

Kindred and *Beloved* both showcase a sort of magical realism but of quite a different type than Gabriel García Márquez (*One Hundred Years of Solitude*, 1970) or Carlos Fuentes (*Where the Air is Clear*, 1960). In fact, Butler described *Kindred* as a "dark fantasy" rather than science fiction (unnamed psi forces trigger time travel) while *Beloved* is a supernatural horror rendered even more horrific by its basis in a possible reality. Both books blend supernatural and fantastic realism with hard social analysis. Both are well-researched in regards to customs, traditions, food, clothing, laws, and speech of the time and place. Both leave the reader wondering uneasily, "But what if it really did happen?"

Subject

Soul-killing humiliation, violence, and degradation within the North American slave system and its lingering affect on the psyches and physical health of the women who endured the pain link the two works.

According to Butler, she initiated the writing of *Kindred* in response to the comment of a friend that unfairly judged black people in the past by current standards, failing to acknowledge their effort to survive in a harsher society. "I think people really need to think what it's like to have all of society arrayed against you. People may think things are that way now, but it was much worse then – it was OK to rape black women because black women couldn't be raped. And it was also OK to kill black people. I wanted to put readers there so they could feel how scary that was and reflect on how to protect yourself when it is legal to mistreat you in so many ways." (*Seattle Post Intelligencer*, 2004)

In *Kindred*, Dana, a modern, well-educated woman living in 1976 Los Angeles with her white husband, Kevin, finds herself called back to nineteenth-century Maryland by a mysterious pull from her white ancestor, Rufus, who needs her to save his life five times during the course of the book. Each call by Rufus places Dana's life and physical well-being in jeopardy. To survive, Dana adjusts her behavior to outwardly conform to that of a black female slave with all the consequences that come with that station in life.

The reader learns from Dana exactly how the white population conditioned slaves with an entire social and legal system poised to enforce the slave's submission to inferior status. A free black woman, who helps her slave husband to escape is herself enslaved for the effort and sold away from her husband, but not before the slave-catchers mutilate him.
The black male slave who defends his free-born wife from sexual attack by a white man loses her to that man through legal cruelty of the time. The slave owner who discovers Dana teaching a slave to read beats Dana. When Dana tries to run away to find her husband, Kevin, the white master of the plantation beats her again.

Within the Introduction, Morrison revealed that the motivation for *Beloved* stemmed from the news clipping of an actual event where a young mother, Margaret Garner, was arrested for killing her child rather than allowing her child to be enslaved. "...So I would invent her thoughts, plumb them for a subtext that was historically true in essence, but not strictly factual in order to relate her history to contemporary issues about freedom, responsibility, and women's 'place.' The heroine would represent the unapologetic acceptance of shame and terror; assume the consequences of choosing infanticide; claim herown freedom." (*Beloved*, 1987).

Sethe, although not the title character, is the central character around whom most of the terrible events in *Beloved* revolve. An ex-slave from Sweet Home plantation in Kentucky, Sethe lives in a two-story house in 1873 Ohio ten years after the formal abolishment of slavery. The two-year-old daughter she killed with a saw to the throat a month after her escape from Sweet Home haunts the house. This supernatural force drives out Sethe's two sons and the family dog leaving just Sethe and Denver to endure the madness until Paul D, another ex-slave from the same plantation arrives. The Fugitive Slave Bill, allowing slave masters to reclaim their runaway "property," shadows the story.

Bad Things

In *Kindred*, Rufus and his father point loaded guns at Dana. Rufus's father strips Dana naked in front of other slaves, ties her wrists above her head, and beats her with rawhide. An overseer beats Dana with a whip for moving too slow in the cornfield. By using physical pain and threat of physical pain to herself and others, Dana's white masters force her to relinquish overt expressions of individuality and humanity. Dana's husband loses five years of his life in the past and also overtly conforms to the antebellum slave system as a white man while secretly working as an Underground Railroad conductor. Dana manipulates Alice into to submitting to rape by Rufus in an effort to protect Alice from a beating and to ensure her own survival as Alice's descendant resulting from the rape. *Kindred* features the sole white woman of the story as having a poor character complete with drug-addled whining petulance, outright hostility, and a willingness to sell slaves and break up families in order to pay for household furnishings.

In *Beloved*, Sethe's white master coolly takes notes while two other white men "milk" her like an animal, stealing her daughter's breast milk. Sethe's husband, hiding in the hayloft watches the sexual assault and slowly goes mad as he realizes he is powerless to protect her. So pregnant Sethe flees slavery alone to reach her children who already escaped while her husband allows darkness to overtake him. The white master kills or sells the other slaves who attempted to escape. The white master then tracks Sethe down a month later with the law in tow and moves to take her and her children back to the plantation. Sethe kills one child (*Beloved*) with the saw, wounds her two boys, and attempts to kill Denver, the youngest daughter. Sethe endures years of spiteful revenge by the murdered child's ghost followed by a physical manifestation of the child that drains Sethe's life force. Morrison reveals other examples of rape and torture forced on slaves including a man who allows his master to rape his wife in order to keep himself and her alive. Another man's master forces him to wear a bit like a horse as punishment for trying to escape. Within *Beloved*, the role of the sole white woman at Sweet Home is that of false sympathy and passive acceptance along with the pragmatic willingness to sell slaves and break-up families in order to ensure her own economic wherewithal. The complete flip side to Sethe's white mistress is the indentured white woman who helps Sethe to give birth to Denver during Sethe's harrowing escape to freedom.

Dangerous Choices

Both Butler and Morrison illustrate that black female slaves made practical choices to negotiate the slave system in order to protect their own lives and the lives of their husbands and children. As Harriet Jacobs described in her narrative, morality was a luxury afforded only to those in a position of power to protect and enforce it. Butler and Morrison also reveal that some slaves chose to die by either murder or suicide rather than face these dilemmas. Many other slaves, imitating the Founding Fathers of North America, decided that most laws regarding slavery needed to be broken and broke them.

Madness

In *Kindred*, Alice, the free black woman sold into slavery for helping her husband to escape offsets Dana's twentieth-century assessment of systematic nineteenth-century efforts to degrade black people. Driven to near insanity and suicide by her dismal circumstances, Alice realizes she has no escape, unlike Dana. Dana, herself, teeters close to the brink of accepting the slave mentality until she takes the initiative to manipulate both Rufus and the psi force that sends her forward in time to safety. Finally, she kills Rufus and completely ends his hold over her.

In *Beloved*, Sethe, driven to near insanity and murder, counters Denver, her remaining daughter, who tries to endure the horror of her mother's actions and the disruptive reappearance of her dead sister, Beloved. In the midst of the tension between Sethe and Beloved, Denver finds the inner-strength to take the initiative to seek help for herself and Sethe from the community that turned its back on them all [those] years before.

Both books show the physical, economic, social, and cultural degradation that resulted from humans treating other humans more cruelly than animals.

At the end of *Kindred*, Dana bears physical evidence of her trauma in the form of missing teeth and a missing lower arm. At the end of *Beloved*, Sethe still has not completely recovered her faculties and bears whip marks or "chokecherry tree" scars on her back. In addition, spiritual, emotional, and mental degradation exemplify the true horror and darkness of slavery since these wounds remained internal, perhaps eternal, and certainly harder to heal. For these reasons, the pleasantly innocuous single-word titles of both stories take on sinister double meanings that jab at the reader now and then.

Stature

Octavia Butler commented on the presence of black people in mainstream literature and her own role as a black author. "What it really means is that to be black is to be abnormal. The norm is white, apparently, in the view of people who see things in that way. For them the only reason you would introduce a black character is to introduce this kind of abnormality. Usually, it's because you're telling a story about racism or at least about race... What I want to do is pull in some good black writers who will write about black people and not just about how terrible it is to be hated." (*Contemporary Authors Online*, 2001)

Kindred proved hard for publishers to categorize. According to Butler, one publisher suggested that she market the book as juvenile literature. After a surprising number of rejections, Doubleday published and marketed *Kindred* as a mainstream novel. Many readers consider it to be her most accessible work although *Parable of the Sower* and *Parable of the Talents* (which won the Nebula Award) benefit from a similar reader friendliness.

Butler enjoys wide recognition in the white, male-dominated field of science fiction and cult status among African American women as well as appreciation by feminists who relate to the gender, power, and social themes definitive of her body of work. Beacon Hill Press selected *Kindred* for a 25th anniversary reprint in 2004.

Toni Morrison also commented on her writing and its role in mainstream literature, offering no apology. "I never asked Tolstoy to write for me, a little colored girl in Lorain, Ohio. I never asked [James] Joyce not to mention Catholicism or the world of Dublin. Never. And I don't know why I should be asked to explain your life to you. We have splendid writers to do that, but I am not one of them... Faulkner wrote what I suppose could be called regional literature and had it published all over the world... From my perspective there are only black people. When I say 'people,' that's what I mean." (*Contemporary Authors Online*, 2005)

Morrison's previous literary endeavors, plus established position within literary circles as English professor and book editor meant *Beloved* did not endure a stream of rejections prior to publication. Critical acclaim from the literary community in the form of prestigious awards brought *Beloved* to even wider attention years after publication, particularly when Oprah Winfrey chose to make the book into a feature film. *Beloved* is universally celebrated as high art.

Music

If books were music, then *Beloved* would play like jazz. A frightening blend of complex layers of artistry that repeated, shifted, repeated, doubled back, allowed the lead vocalist a chance to shine, then brought in the keyboards, then the bass and guitar, then the horns, all backed by the percussion that beat a steady, rhythmic, hypnotizing heartbeat in the background. The music would swell, quiet, swell, quiet, swell, crescendo, then end, leaving nothing but an empty echo surrounding the audience who wondered what on Earth did they just hear? And when, oh when, would the band gig again?

And if *Beloved* played like jazz, then *Kindred* would answer with the blues. A direct onslaught of shock, pain, suffering, and wonder at this crazy world. The lead vocalist would take center stage with nothing but guitar in hand and wail out starkly simple phrases backed by riffs that demanded complete attention and focus. The vocalist would yank the audience by the collar, make the audience gasp at the outrage, then speed them along to the climax. Exhausted at the finish, both the vocalist and audience feel completely justified by the intense expression of their feelings. And then the audience would finally understand a reality gone completely out of control.

Is *Beloved* a better-written, more profound fictionalization of the slave narrative than *Kindred*? To answer would be akin to making a decision between jazz and blues, trying to decide which style is "better." Both music styles are uniquely North American with enduring influence on today's most popular music styles – country and rock, hip hop and R&B/soul. In the same way, both *Kindred* and *Beloved* serve North American and world readers with an intimately personal exploration of the most uniquely peculiar institution ever created to found a nation and the price that entire nation still pays for the atrocity. The very fact that both Toni Morrison and Octavia Butler created these works, published them, distributed them, and contributed their historical explorations to high school and college curricu[la], reveals that despite the dark legacies of horrific history, the books forthrightly speak aloud the unspeakable and rest their spines alongside the works of other classic North American literature such as *The Handmaid's Tale* (Margaret Atwood, 1985), *Absalom! Absalom!* (William Faulkner, 1936), and *The Confessions of Nat Turner* (William Styron, 1968), in addition to other titles mentioned in this essay.

Resouces

Bloom, Harold. Editor. *Toni Morrison (Modern Critical Views)*. Chelsea House Publishers. 1990.

Butler, Octavia. *Kindred*. Doubleday. 1979

Butler, Octavia. *Kindred*. Beacon Press. 1988

Morrison, Toni. B*eloved*. Knopf. 1987

"Octavia E(stelle) Butler." *Contemporary Authors Online*. Thomas Gale. Last updated 05/04/2001. *Accessed 01/03/2006.*

Marshall, John. "Pioneering sci-fi writer Octavia Butler has overcome many barriers and hardships." *Seattle Post-Intelligencer*. February 16, 2004.

"Toni Morrison." *Contemporary Authors Online*. Thomas Gale. Last Updated 09/28/05. *Accessed 12/31/2005.*

On Street K

[from *Imaginarium*, 2006]

In my dreams I visited that place
I saw and walked away
Nightmare and vision of K Street
I saw and walked away

A little boy leads me to the door
I look back on it today
Turns and points and grins to show
That everything's okay

Drug dealers, pimps, and their customers
Argue over the pay
Half-naked hookers scream obscenities
I heard and chose to stay

The place police no longer police
Once the sun goes away
The man at the door is surprised at me
His face turns completely gray

He gestures at me whispering, "Just leave
And for your life pray!"
The package I borrowed, I set it down
The boy waves me away

So down the stairs I'm lucky for my life
But I'm late for Society Soirée
And what should I do, a stranger there?
My journey is home and holiday

For his disobedience, for forgetting the rule
On the window ledge he lays
The boy, that boy who helped me there
Screams, "I didn't betray!"

They hold him by his feet... for a while
Because I saw and so did they
The next window up high, a punishment
A little girl's skin they flay

I saw it. I heard it.
And yet, I walked away
I valued my life. I wanted to live.
And so, I walked away.

The neighborhood stopped, frozen, shocked
And watched the entire little play
On this street in filmed slow motion
Voyeur's Lunatic Matinee

The third window up high another child up there
This is the price that they pay
The price for doing things... unasked
They are examples to display

To the next street and the next block
I stumbled far, far away
Keeping straight remaining neutral
Saving only my own life, to my dismay

Who am I? Who are you?
I'm just... trying to convey
I saw it all. I saw all of it.
I admit that I was there that day

No siren no whistle
Just me walking away
I am them. They are me.
But I walked away

Court to cell it happens to us
Behind these bars, here to stay
They all shout. They try me.
But I never look away

Outside my cell now I walk towards the yard
Two hours of sun today
My accusers grip my wrists hard
Against the steel and say

"You saw our children. You did nothing.
You go the exact same way.
The children are gone and now so are you
You see Death come today."

I went to that place that godless place
I saw and I walked away
But it's over now. I no longer dream
Of what I saw on Street K

Dreams

[from _Celara Sun_, 2010]

I took my dreams off the wall
So I would not see what I had not done

I took my dreams out of my mouth
So I would not voice those untruths

I took my dreams out of my ears
Because I did not want to hear them lie to me

I took my dreams out of my mind
While I slept, they tortured me

I pretended my dreams do not exist
And I breathed so free

I put my dreams on this page
Now I hold you captive to my dreams

When We Were Greens
[McQueen Press Official Website, 2010]

We need to bring green back. Today. We need to bring health and wealth back. Now. At very little cost. More than that, we should hire our own grandparents and great grandparents as consultants to advise us how to do it.

Why?

Because they were green before it was a notion. They were green when it was called common sense!

Who better than a man or woman who survived the Great Depression, World Wars, Jim Crow, the Civil Rights Movement, and persistent institutional backlash against economic achievement to show us the road to a sustainable lifestyle?

The answers have been rocking in their chairs, playing chess, sitting on the porch, and shaking their heads at the younger generations for years!

For instance, one set of my grandparents lived in a rural region and owned and operated a sorghum mill, maintained vast fruit and nut orchards, raised timber and other cash crops, and raised enormous kitchen gardens of vegetables and herbs. They also bred horses and raised chickens, cows, and pigs. They hunted game and fished. They were organic and free-range and biodynamic decades before these words became Internet search terms.

That was a lot of work! Who did it? Their children!

Social, political, and economic upheavals came and went. My grandparents maintained what they owned through humble spirits, generosity, strong community ties, and strong work ethics.

My other set of grandparents, who lived a tad more urban lifestyle, turned on a dime when it came to energy-efficiency and recycling. Oh *yes!*

Though they lived in the city, my other grandparents had a system that worked. My grandfather learned the carpentry and electrical trades. In fact, he was a genius who built, invented, and repaired his own home and those of his neighbors as well as people in the city who needed a job done right and well. Railroad and construction jobs were available often, but not always. So his two most lucrative assets remained his own two hands. I loved to see what new contraptions he rigged in the house and the backyard to make his work easier and the utility bill lesser.

My grandmother found at least five uses for the same glass jar, rubber band, plastic jug, pantyhose, and random metal machine part that found its way into their home. She did not throw old clothes away. She sliced off the buttons, zippers, and other useful pieces for future sewing projects. Whatever was leftover became a household rag or something with which she tied up tomatoes. She grew herbs for her bath, cosmetics, and medicine.

This set of grandparents also had chickens and gathered their own eggs for breakfast. I never saw either of them eat fast food. Instead, a selection of not locally-grown, but *home-grown* balanced meals hit the table at high noon each day. I actually tried to time my grandmother a few times to see how she managed to get everything just right at the same time everyday, but she shooed me out of the kitchen, so I can't tell you.

Basically, my grandparents learned to make something out of nothing--the ultimate philosophy in sustainable living.

We need to bring green back. Not because it is popular, but because our health, wealth, and spirit depend upon it.

It is not exotic or foreign to go green. It is not expensive to go green. It is common sense to go green.

Grow organic gardens on raised beds in the back yard, front porch, sunny room in house, kitchen window, garage, church yard, or vacant lot.

Compost kitchen and lawn plant refuse.

Use rain barrels. They'll fill up fast!

Dechemicalize the home with baking soda, lemon juice, vinegar, and beeswax substitutes for household cleansers.

Try a caulking gun!

Sew your own clothes.

Create your own soap, candles, perfumes, and lotions with your own spices and herbs.

Dare I say reconsider expensive salon visits in favor of natural hairstyles?

Handle stress with adrenaline and endorphins from exercise rather than excess food, drugs, and liquor. Thoughts become clearer. Purpose becomes greater.

Get those children off the Internet, the game system, and the television. Their energy, positivity, and ability to learn new ideas quickly are greatly needed to assist your new grandparent consultants in building your new greenhouse!

We all have the talent and skill to bring green back. We just require the will. Where there is a will, there is a way.

Just ask the elder in your house to unlock the secrets stored away from childhood and then point the way.

Silk and Silver

[from *Sudan: The Lion of Truth*, 2nd ed, 2011]

I adored you in silk and silver
The words you said
The way they slithered
How I shook
How I shivered
The way you made
Me always quiver
And I always came
Softly back for more
Skin thirsty
I adored
Silk and silver

Breakaway

[from *Windrunner*, 2012]

Thinking about it everyday
Letting those thoughts slip away

Eternal Searcher waits for you.

You are the Sky.
I am the Blue.

Reverie

[from *Road Romance: Tales from the Book Tour*, 2013]

Day dreams of greens and pinks
Lost in thought
And revelry
Of blue on blue silver
And trees, and flowers, and springs
And windmills and water towers
And red barns and brown grass and sweet rocks
Misty rain
Dreams while I wake
Musings while I walk
Sleep never
Just always, Reverie

The Ship of Fools
[from the *Dark Fantastic: 12 Short Screenplays*, 2013]

The Seeker
Went out
But never returned
So they sent
Another one

This ship of fools
Followed The Seeker
And found Cruel World
Not foreign
Alien

The warning beacon cried
Fear, pain, death
Unspeakable
Unexplainable
Inhuman

A world where
Humans are the pets
Cattle
Product
Food

Arrogant on Earth
Subjugated on
Cruel World
Reduced to
Humiliation

The caste system
The aliens created
Abominable
Indescribable
Suicidal

The Seeker
Is gone
Of the ship of fools
Only two remain
Alive

But not alive
Comatose
Male and female
Locked together
Tethered

Forced to
Reproduce like
Beasts
For the aliens
Cattle

Years go by
The humans
Reproduce and
Provide more humans
For alien harvest

Before the slaughter
Before the cages
The ship of fools
Sent another beacon
To warn Earth

About the cages
Locked into place
Like beasts
Forced to rape
Each other

Mothers and sons
Fathers and daughters
Sisters and brothers
The aliens
Did not care

They feed the humans
Breed the humans
Harvest the humans
Eat the humans
Wear the humans

Two humans
Remain in stasis
Alive
But not Alive
Aware

Screaming
Insanity
Praying for
Heart attacks
Now comatose

Milk, Blood, Semen
Urine, Saliva, Skin
The aliens
Find uses
For everything

The alien race
Will increase
Their herd of
Earth beasts and
Earth meat

But will it ever
Be enough?
Because of The Seeker
And the Ship of Fools
The aliens know Earth

Cruel World
They like us
They want us
They want more
They will find us

Dreams in Arkana
[from *The Cadis Evening*, 2016]

The long night is over
Or is it
The nightmare has ended
Or has it
Light fills the empty space
Or does it
Dreams in Arkana

Writing Influences
[McQueen Press YouTube Channel, 2016]

Hi everybody. It's Lee McQueen of McQueen Press. I'm just signing in again, to continue the discussion of my writing and what it means to me.

This segment, I'm gonna be discussing my writing influences. My latest work is *The Cadis Evening*. It's this work right here. Paperback. Thirty chapters. It's a suspense novel. I just completed it this past May. I'm super-excited about that work because it's a culmination of everything I've learned about writing so far.

These are my other works behind me. Short story collection. There's a poetry collection which is now out of print. And then there's also a couple of novels I've written, and a couple of non-fictions screenplays. Writing for me is not a chore, it's a joy. And so, hopefully, I'll be working on something else very soon. I'm thinking it's gonna be another collection of screenplays. I've got three ready to go. They're short screenplays. Three of them are ready to go, and I'm thinking that work is also gonna include storyboards. I give into the joy of writing. And I keep going.

But now, I'm wanting to discuss some of my writing influences that I've developed and that I've gravitated towards over the years. And I tried to make a list as tight and concise as I could which is recommended for writing. But I couldn't get it as short as I planned. I wanted to do just my top three and I just said I can't get it down to three. So, I'll just run through some names. And maybe say a little bit of what that author means to me and why that work speaks to me.

First, I've got Edgar Allen Poe. It almost goes without saying, he's one of our great North American writers. The thing with him is he wasn't afraid to go into the darkness. Which is a scary place. Even though some of his works are horrific in nature, it's mostly kind of in his head kind of horror. Where it's like psychological, where you're thinking, did it really happen? Was it all a dream? And then, also, not only to dark places without, but also within. In his poetry, in his short stories, and then in his novels as well. And so, that's why I'm really fascinated by Edgar Allen Poe.

I actually tried to write a poem along the lines of "The Raven," but I couldn't do it. He's just so great and so original that I said, I can never write a poem like him, but I can write a poem inspired by him. And I did that, and it's called "On Street K," where I explored the darkness that I've seen. Or that I knew about. Or that resonated with me, rather than borrowing someone else's dreams and fantasies. That's why I really enjoy the work of Edgar Allen Poe.

I'll even say that, because there are some other dark writers on this list, but, one of the darkest books ever written is the "Book of Revelations" from the *Bible*. And some of the worst nightmares in literature have been inspired by the darkness contained in the "Book of Revelations." And so, horror as a literary art has a very significant presence in the world of writing.

Okay. My other choice was Nathaniel Hawthorne. Another classic, romantic writer in North America. Particularly, finding the darkness in the ordinary, we'll say. Just ordinary people and the horror that lays under their lives. Almost, how people treat each other in an ordinary community. One of my favorite stories by Nathaniel Hawthorne, is not actually *The Scarlet Letter*. It's a short story he wrote called "Rappuccini's Daughter." And I'll just let the viewer of this video follow up on that. You'll probably see what I'm talking about after you read it. That he even thought to write something like that. But he's a great writer.

My other choice is H.G. Wells, science fiction author, who's written so many fantastic science fiction stories that have an element of technology or steam punk. Or a fascination with the mechanics of science fiction. And so, him, along with Jules Verne, it was almost a choice of well you can go with H.G. Wells or Jules Verne. For this list, I chose H.G. Wells. There's so many titles by him that I really really enjoy.

C.S. Lewis is one of my very favorite authors. I love him and his work so much. As a child, I read the *Narnia* series. And, didn't quite pick up that it was biblical until I was a little bit older. Which goes to show what a great writer he was that he was able to engage a young reader without pounding over the head with biblical morality or moralizing. It was just plain good writing. As I got older, I graduated more towards the *Perelandra* series. Where there's the travel to the moon. No. Yeah. I think it's the moon [it's actually Mars]. And then also to Venus. And the science behind that and then just the writing style itself. I really enjoy C.S. Lewis.

Really high on my list, and this goes back to where I can't choose just one. I just love everyone so much. But Octavia Butler is a personal hero of mine. And I say this even as one of the biggest fan girls of Octavia Butler. I happened to meet her. I was very privileged to have met her almost ten years ago. When she was doing a book tour in support of *Fledgling*, her vampire book.

But she's also explored time travel and, let's see, time travel, oh yeah, and the Xenogenisis and the genetic manipulation type of books. The mind magic books. With the *Wild Seed*. Her writing style just blows my mind. She set no limits for herself. She rolled with the big boys in terms of science fiction. And so I really value her as a writer very much.

To this day, I'm just so puzzled as to why there have been so many post-apocalyptic movies that have been released in the theaters, but not one has included her *Parable* series. *The Parable of the Talents* or *The Parable of the Sower*. And even when we had the vampire craze, like post-*Blade*, she wrote her *Fledgling* book and that could have easily been made into a movie. Or even *Kindred*, the time travel book, using psi energy. I'm still waiting for that. I'm hoping, and someday soon, maybe we'll see that.

Moving along on my list, Ben Bova and Kim Stanley Robinson, have written a lot of space opera and space travel books. Imagining a society far into the future where space travel is an ordinary thing. Like going to the other side of the Earth, like from here to Australia. They imagine space travel that way where there's a lot of interplanetary travel and the political aspects of that and terraforming. Things that happen in an inter-planetary society. Particularly, Kim Stanley Robinson, his gift for description and world building. I really admire his use of language.

Isaac Asimov is very high on my list. He's high on a lot of people's lists. I like his *Robot* series. His short stories. I find his work imaginative. I've often tried, again with Edgar Allen Poe, I tried to pattern myself after him. But not copy. You can't copy Isaac Asimov. But he has inspired a lot of my work in *Imaginarium*, my short stories.

I read a short story from Isaac Asimov, I think it was just one page long. And I cannot tell you the title, it's so long ago. But I said, I'm gonna try that. I'm gonna write a short story that is exactly one page long. I'm gonna try to do it. And, I managed to do it. And, I said that was a good exercise for me to learn from greatness. And, try to be great myself, while I'm at it.

Let's see, who else do I have on my list? I've got Linda Howard and I've got Jayne Anne Krentz. These are romance writers, I would say. But genre romance writers. Jayne Anne Krentz writes a lot of romance with an aspect of the supernatural. Or romance involving talented people who have powers. I enjoy her writing style. Her dialogue, particularly, I find wonderful to read and to use as inspiration for myself. Her regency series. And then just the gift of humor between characters, I think that's great.

Linda Howard, she writes suspense romance. Romance suspense. I just like her plots that she comes up with. And the aspect of thrills involving the female character who's often the center of the action and saving the world. Or something like that.

Agatha Christie is also on this list. I am not a mystery writer. I've tried to write one mystery and I didn't enjoy it, so I didn't finish it. I'll read a mystery, but I don't like to write a mystery. And the mystery I really started off reading is Agatha Christie. And, a lot of people like Agatha Christie. She's still a best-selling author, I believe, to this day for her large catalog of work. And I believe I've managed each and every one of her works. But I keep hoping that I've missed one. And maybe there's an Agatha Christie I haven't read. And I'll have a chance to read another. But, I think I've covered them all.

Finally, adding on my list, Jim Butcher. And, I almost tried to not add him on. But I just love his writing style so much. Even though I've told myself over and over that I'm not a fan of fantasy. That I struggle with fantasy because I prefer science fiction. But, I have to say that once I picked up Jim Butcher's wizard series. The wizard, I believe his name is Harry and he's a wizard detective in Chicago. And I just could not put it down. He's got everything from dragons to dinosaurs, I believe, and fairies. And of course wizards and vampires running around in his books. But, I just like it. The writing, and I just can't stop. And it's funny. I think there was a television series and I didn't get to see. But, I like his wizard series.

And so to sum up, there's a lot of genre fiction that I'm interested in. Everything from mystery to science fiction with a little bit of fantasy. And how it influenced my work is also not allowing myself to be limited. And to really exploring the world as it looks to me. And even beyond the immediate world into a hyper-fantastic reality of what the world looks like to me. And so, my own work is not too spacey, or out there, or too far from the norm. But it's more of imagining the ordinary, and then adding layers of hyper-reality or hyper-fantasy onto that.

And I did forget one of my favorite authors and that's Stephen King. Sometimes, it's funny when you tell people, I like Stephen King. They think, oh, he writes crazy stuff. He writes dark horrific stuff. He is a wonderful writer. Stephen

King is probably one of the greatest writers we have engaged in the business here in North America, right now. It might be that he's our modern-day Edger Allen Poe or Nathaniel Hawthorne who's with us right now to enjoy. Some of his writing, of course, has been off-putting for content. But his writing style, his original plots, his willingness to go where people fear to tread puts him up right up there with the greatest writers, I think, of all time. No, he's not the greatest writer. Because, who knows? There might be one that's born tomorrow, and then *he's* the greatest writer. But he is one *of* the greatest writers. His vast catalog, his many sales, the many steps into other genres like movies, and plays, and screenplays and short stories, that he's written in, I think that's terrific. It's just sharing the gift a different way. I believe lately, he's writing police procedurals. Who saw that coming? I've read a couple of those and I enjoyed those. But, I think overall he's just a terrific writer. No one can tell a story like Stephen King can.

And so, I've learned a lot from the people that I've read. And it's almost like when you read a book, and you're a writer, that's your education. A writer writes, of course. But a writer also reads. And so, I'm a heavy reader and a heavy writer. I'm slowly building up my catalog. But I likely will never stop learning from other authors. And then hopefully, other people might pick up my books and maybe learn something from me.

I mentioned the *Bible* earlier and I wanted to come back to it, because I do think that is the greatest story ever told. And there's a reason why the *Bible* is the highest most selling books of all time. And it's still a best seller. It's just one of the greatest books ever written. And I say that not because I'm trying to recruit you to my or another religion. But just even from a literary aspect, you read the "Book of Proverbs," or the "Psalms," or the writing of the "Song of Solomon," and the writing is so poetic and so magical that that's also one of those books that you can't put down.

So, I learn quite a lot from a lot of different sources. Even just reading the newspaper, I pick up story ideas all the time.

But yes, reading is a pleasure and so is writing. And I think they go hand-in-hand.

Thank you!

Viewpoints

[official positions, 2018]

Healthcare

Single-payer healthcare is the fiscally-conservative solution to the multiple healthcare failures and debacles of the recent past as proven by economist Gerald Friedman. With single payer, everyone has healthcare (including general, dental, vision, mental, long-term, reproductive, pediatric) regardless of income level, pre-existing conditions, age, employment status, geography, etc.

Everyone already has universal access to police, fire, military defense, national guard, parks, libraries, streets, emergency services, disaster relief so it makes sense to add healthcare to the list of services guaranteed by the federal government. Everyone pays a small tax, they same way everyone pays for other government-guaranteed services. Because the pool of inclusion is so large, the risk and cost goes down. There are no premiums, deductibles, co-pays, or overages because there is no corporate profiteering.

Small businesses benefit from government-guaranteed healthcare because single payer takes the burden off small business owners to constrict expansion of their businesses, allowing them to spend more time and energy on their bottom line rather than insurance administration.

Private health insurers are unnecessary and unwelcome, rather they are dangerous, to required and preventative care. The role of private health insurance is to provide coverage for supplemental or recreational healthcare.

Women's reproductive healthcare

Our U.S. Congress and state legislatures are composed primarily of lawyers who have no medical training, medical experience, medical degrees, or medical licenses. Practicing medicine without a license is considered a crime most of the time.

Those without professional medical degrees and licenses have NO BUSINESS interfering with medical treatment provided by trained, licensed professionals. NO BUSINESS denying medical treatment and procedures recommended by trained, licensed professionals. NO BUSINESS violating HIPAA and other privacy laws.

Medical treatment and procedures are the provenance of the patients and their physicians who have direct access to their medical histories and medical charts, not random members of the state legislature, governor, random members of Congress, Vice-President, or President who all feel a ludicrous need to showboat with ignorance and arrogance in the delivery of life or death, personal and private medical services.

Family planning education, birth control/prevention, family support, economic justice are preferred methods to address maternal and infant mortality rates rather than criminalization, harassment, and intimidation of, as well as violence towards women.

Family support

"Family values" means actual support of family units with vacation, sick and family leave, and *not* the discipline and punishment of women and children.

The United States stands alone as the only nation in the developed world that has no policy for paid family leave. Perhaps because of the "rugged individualism" dream of a long-ago frontier life that has resulted in increased maternal and infant mortality rates in modern times.

Civilized nations nurture and raise their young. A nation of barbarians refuses to nurture and raise their young. Paid family leave is a policy with multi-partisan support and prevents dependence upon social welfare programs. Provide parental leave for six months for both parents. Provide affordable, universal, federally-funded childcare and daycare.

Expand the Earned Income Tax Credit to provide additional support to families with children to offset regressive payroll taxes.

"Rugged individualism" is not even a guiding concept for our military troops who value teamwork over self-glory. We as a society would benefit from a higher value given to the common sense concept of community.

Prescription Drugs research and retail

The single payer, the U.S. government, needs to step forward *right now* to confront multi-national pharmaceutical corporations from further exploiting and harming consumers. Negotiate prices to a reasonable, common sense level. Cut subsidies to Big Pharma corporations who use those subsidies for advertising and lobbying (bribing) members of the U.S. Congress rather than on actual research and development.

Public Education

Control over the future of the public school system is being fought in North America. Wealthy individuals, organizations, and corporations view public schools and their students as sources of profit, as consumers, and as inventory in a captured capitalistic market system. Some term this type of predatory capitalism upon children as "reform" and "choice." Corporate profiteering upon our youth is neither reform nor choice.

Some of America's wealthiest citizens back school board candidates, even in states in which they don't reside such as

Louisiana, California, Minnesota, Washington, and yes, Arkansas, too. The goal is to push the oligarchal point-of-view of how public schools should operate or not operate.

Dark money, flows into school elections. Oligarchs donate to nonprofit organizations that spend that dark money in order to influence elections and public policy without disclosure. These dark money candidates support the destruction of the public school system. They support privatization, charter schools, evaluating teachers by test score rather than actual performance. The sole goal of these "reformers" is to privatize public education.

Holding the line against predatory capitalism upon children, are parents, teachers, and students themselves who fight to protect the future leaders of North America.

To counter-act overwhelming exposure, promotion, and celebration of violence in mass media, public schools administrators should require the teaching non-violent conflict resolution and humane education at all levels of education.

Private, for-profit entities like Big Pharma and soft drink companies should have no provenance over decision-making for local public school systems. Instead, public schools administrators should ensure the provision of healthy school meals to students with the assistance of Farm-to-School programs which provide food from local family farms and vocational and nutritional education opportunities.

The United States should join the rest of the world in setting eighteen years as the absolute minimum age for military recruitment. Our students and their records should be protected from access by military recruiters.

Pre-K education, vocational education, sports programs and physical education, plus music and arts education must be maintained. If we do not capture and develop the minds of our children early, they become vulnerable to other educational influences–consumerism, violence, depression, apathy.

Federal policy is required to assist parents and teachers in ensuring equal access to quality public education and to eliminate inequalities in school funding at the local and state level. Separate but equal is inherently, unequal.

Teachers and counselors should be treated and compensated as education professionals rather than undermined by volunteers and interns to the detriment of actual curriculum development and classroom management which are professional skills.

Our children and youth are not captured corporate markets. Neither are they inventory for corporate exploitation, including the school to private, for-profit prison pipeline.

Instead, the candidate supports the Youth Jobs Program proposed by Sen. Bernie Sanders. This $5.5 billion program would create 1 million jobs for disadvantaged young Americans. Paid for by ending the carried interest loophole that allows billionaire hedge fund managers to pay a lower tax rate than nurses, teachers, and truck drivers.

It is time to repeal the No Child Left Behind Act and cease "teaching to the test."

Free college tuition

Senator Bernie Sanders:

"...the devastating burden of high student debt not only causes enormous financial problems for individuals and families, it also destroys dreams."

We as a nation can afford to send our youth to institutions of higher education without breaking their spirits, without mortgaging their futures, and acting as financial predators upon their future happiness. Every species on Earth endures by nurturing their young rather than by preying upon and devouring their young.

We have the financial means with which to accomplish free higher education going forward, including 4-year universities, community colleges, vocational schools, as well as forgiveness of existing student loan debt, if we cease subsidizing military over-expansion and corporate welfare to dinosaur industries. Instead, expand higher education. A tax on Wall Street transactions is another method for a federal program. Some states have used their lotteries to fund college tuition.

In the true spirit of rehabilitation, prisoners must have academic and vocational education and training in the effort to avoid repeat offenses and recidivism and to protect communities.

Arkansas has made headway in offering free community college tuition as well as free college and university tuition to students over 60-years old, but we can and should raise our expectations and go nationwide with free college tuition for all.

Funds for local community centers

Isolated strangers log off the Internet and disrupt their solitude in order to walk through streets and parks, share information, exchange ideas, eat, fellowship, listen to music, and learn about each others lives. Soon, these people become actual "neighbors and friends." Farmers markets, park events, and street parties provide similar methods to recognize that humans are meant to be social and thrive when together!

New industries

Legalize industrial hemp for textile use. Regulate and tax hemp like potatoes, rice, cotton, wheat, soybeans, corn, any other cash crop. Legalize production, processing, and possession of recreational marijuana. Regulate and tax recreational marijuana like alcohol and tobacco.

Launch large-scale renewable energy projects the like to which Arkansas has never before been seen to take advantage of our abundant, but unfortunately under-used solar energy resources. As the state of Iowa has already discovered renewable energies like wind and biomass are critical to improving the farm economy. In other states like Texas and Kentucky, solar has added revenue to rural economies.

Meanwhile, fossil fuel extraction poisons both urban and rural communities. The fuel is exported with no benefit to the communities contaminated along the transportation route. Renewable energy is harder to export, is most often used stateside, and therefore results in true energy independence.

The Clean Line wind transmission project across Northern Arkansas which would have paralleled the Diamond Pipeline fossil fuel pipeline project to connect energy to consumers in Memphis, Tennessee is one example of a better choice unchosen

New jobs

We need to put our people to work as soon as possible, *tomorrow*, on large-scale retrofitting, modernization, streamlining, rebuilding of Arkansas's infrastructure–roads, bridges, sidewalks, bike paths, smart grid electrical transmissions, expansion of broadband and high-speed internet communications networks, public works, waterways.

We need to fill our abandoned industrial parks and buildings with active, thriving manufacturing and production of the parts necessary for renewable energy development and infrastructure modernization. We need service providers and retail workers to provide the end results to the consumers.

Presidential candidate Ross Perot warned this nation about the giant sucking sound of jobs disappearing via misguided trade deals. Fortunately, the Green New Deal jobs, backed by the OFF Fossil Fuels for a Better Future Act, are harder to export and most often remain stateside.

We as a nation and as a state accomplished big jumps in technology and engineering during the Industrial Revolution, the New Deal era, and the WWII era. We are long OVERDUE for another jump into the future. The Future of Arkansas is for All. 4th to the Future!

Local Economy

Allow communities to set higher standards than federal for environment, human rights, labor, consumer, health and safety standards.

Create incentives for co-op enterprises and credit unions.

Invest in the commons like infrastructure, mass transit, and environment by directing newly-created money through public banks which leads to job creation.

Job creation is a method to transfer wealth into the hands of the working and middle class, thereby increasing demand for goods and services, thereby creating more jobs. A 30-35 work week achieves the goal of more job creation. Those who cannot find a livable wage in the private sector should have the opportunity as well as the guarantee of living wage job opportunities in the public sector, which benefits regional economies.

Small businesses should not be hurt by out-of-date zoning ordinances, excessive taxes not paid by large corporations, fees, and bureaucratic burdens. Single payer government-guaranteed healthcare is another method to ease the burden of time, money, and energy expended by small business owners so they can concentrate on expansion of their enterprises.

Renewable energy development and agriculture go hand-in-hand as the state of Iowa has already discovered. In Arkansas, solar energy development is one method to increase revenue for large industrial-scale and family-sized farms, which decreases and perhaps eliminates the need for agricultural subsidies.

NAFTA

Any trade deal (or treaty) that includes the Investor State Dispute Settlement clause is a direct attack upon the U.S. Constitution and is a betrayal of the citizens of the United States. ISDS prevents citizens from using the U.S. judicial system from obtaining remedies for attacks upon civil, human, and labor rights, environmental abuse, and harm to consumers.

Any member of Congress who voted to grant fast-track authority to former President Obama for Transpacific Partnership ratification should be questioned regarding their stance on the renegotiation of NAFTA. An expanded NAFTA that includes specific clauses from the deservedly dead Transpacific Partnership should not be ratified by our U.S. Congress.

Minimum wage

Livable wage should be raised to at least $15/hour, then tied to inflation to keep pace with the rising cost of living. More money circulating in the hands of citizens means a larger middle-class spending on local businesses, buying property/goods/services, creating demand and adding to the tax base for prosperous community development and quality public education.

National Debt

Increase taxes on large corporations, super-rich, polluters and enforce actual payment of those corporate taxes.

Decrease expenditures on war, armaments, corporate welfare. Eliminate subsidies to fossil fuel industries.

No privatization of Social Security.

Increase funding for Green jobs, Social Security, higher education, public transportation, environmental protection, renewable energy, energy efficiency, conservation efforts.

Income/wealth inequality

The UN's Special Rapporteur acknowledged the current, heart-breaking reality of wealth inequality in the U.S.

Supply-side (voodoo) economics does not result in job creation. Rather, supply side economics results in wealthy individuals and large corporations sitting on top of large amounts of wealth, hoarding ill-gotten gains like King Midas, which do not circulate.

Demand-side economics means transferring wealth into the hands of the working and middle class via jobs. This wealth transfer encourages spending on goods and services. Spending on goods and services increases demand. Increased demand promotes job creation and stimulates the economy as money circulates through a prosperous community with a strengthened tax base.

Fair Taxation

Fair taxation is progressive taxation.

We recommend a shift of tax burden from individuals of the working and middle class, plus a shift of tax burden from small businesses towards large corporations which have avoided paying their designated tax rate for decades. Small businesses should not be penalized with the financial burden left to them by large corporations who refuse to pay their fair share.

Most working people pay too much in taxes compared to corporations, multi-millionaires and billionaires. Many of our biggest and most profitable corporations pay little or no taxes. Much investment income is taxed at less than the rate that workers pay. We recommend the elimination of the tax loopholes and exemptions for large corporations and wealthy individuals.

Sales, property, local, other taxes mean that middle and working class people actually pay a higher rate than the 1%. Equalize the equation. Lower these regressive taxes on the working and middle class. Provide the working and middle class with tax rebates, and refunds. Bring corporate taxes into line with world norms and enforce actual collection and payment of that designated tax rate. Slash tax loopholes and giveaways via the tax code. Everyone should pay their fair share.

Simplification of the tax system is strongly recommended.

Corporate Power

Corporate leaders don't just control their corporations, they now exercise control over three branches of government, which is oligarchy, which is unacceptable in a nation that attempts to declare itself a democracy.

The current legal structure of corporations requires profits above all else, including equal protection, equal opportunity, fair play, environment, human rights, public health (for example, Energy Transfer Partners's violent suppression of Standing Rock Sioux Nation and water protectors).

Artificial personhood granted to corporations via Citizens United must be reversed with federal and state constitutional amendments.

Anti-trust laws and regulatory efforts must be strengthened. Corporate charters must strengthen the rights of shareholders to stop corporate abuse. Shareholders should have the right to regulate and reduce excessive executive pay.

States must revoke the charters of those corporations that violate safety, health, environment, human rights laws.

Business regulation

We need to closely examine ineffective regulations that harm small businesses and prevent the small businesses from expanding and growing. Small business expansion is helpful for community prosperity.

Small businesses should not be hurt by out-of-date zoning ordinances, excessive taxes not paid by large corporations, fees, and bureaucratic burdens. However, single payer government-guaranteed healthcare is another method to ease the burden of time, money, and energy expended by small business owners so they can concentrate on expansion of their enterprises.

At the same time, we need to shut the revolving door and maintain distance between regulatory boards and the regulated, never the twain shall meet.

Strengthen the civil justice system to hold corporations liable for corporate crime, fraud, violence, and malfeasance. Revoke the charters of corporations that persistently violate safety, health, environmental protection, or other laws.

Empower shareholders to stop abuses by the managers they hire through a structure of democratic governance and elections.

Enforce existing antitrust laws and support even tougher new ones to curtail the overwhelming economic and political power of large corporations. Increase funding for and strengthen oversight of federal antitrust enforcement.

Insurance Reform

Prohibit price-fixing and avoidance of obligation by private insurers.

Eliminate the for-profit cash money bail system and the ability for private insurers to underwrite those bonds.

Enact single payer healthcare to eliminate private insurer profiteering from death and disease.

Prohibit large companies from being the insurance beneficiaries of their own employees.

Support secondary financial markets that expand credit for economic development, affordable housing, home ownership, sustainable agriculture, rural development, family farms. In other words, reward good behavior.

Banking reform

End tax-payer bailouts of banks insurers, and other financial services institutions. The federal government should not be the guarantor of last resort for irresponsible and risky speculation. At the very least, any federal relief provided should be provided equally at the local level for instance to homeowners and small businesses.

Establish a tax on stock, bond, foreign currency, and financial derivatives transactions to discourage risky and reckless speculation and to generate revenue for nationwide higher and vocational education.

Establish a 10% cap on interest rates above inflation for credit cards, mortgages, payday loans, etc.

Re-enact Glass-Steagall which limited the conflicts of interest created when commercial banks are permitted to underwrite stocks or bonds, and established the FDIC, and strengthened the Federal Reserve's ability to control credit, and prohibited risky economic transactions.

Community Reinvestment Act should be extended with close

scrutiny of foreclosure and anti-redlining laws. Establish a moratorium on fraudulent foreclosures without legal clearance or documentation, specifically for those homes used as the primary residence.

More charter community banks should be capitalized with public funds similar to the stable and financially-solid public Bank of North Dakota that has existed for over one hundred years. Public banks are more profitable, safer, less corrupt, and more accountable overall than private banks. Phil Murphy, himself a former Wall Street banker recently elected to the governor's seat in New Jersey, has indicated his intentions to establish such a public bank for the benefit of citizens and their communities in New Jersey.

Prosecute criminal bank speculation, predatory home loans, large-scale securitization with prison terms, revocation of charter, seizure of assets.

I recommend forgiveness of all student and parent loans for post-secondary and vocational education. The approximately $40 billion required is a fraction of the cost used to bailout the big banks and to create the latest financial war package.

Money reform

Nationalize the twelve reserve banks and reconstitute them under a new Monetary Board Authority under the U.S. Treasury. Stop allowance of the private creation of money by private banks rather than public banks.

Privatized control of the money system has led to irresponsible speculation, toxic loans, and phony financial instruments and has created no real wealth or jobs.

Governments must take back the special money creation privilege from private banks. The Monetary Board Authority, FDIC, SEC, U.S. Treasury, Congressional Budget Office, must redefine bank lending rules, end private bank money creation, and the fractional reserve system.

Spend newly-created money into circulation by directing those funds through community banks like Bank of North Dakota and interest-free loans to local/state entities for infrastructure modernization, health projects, education, etc. The American Society of Civil Engineers has already stated the need for $2.2 trillion for our nationwide infrastructure needs, which can be accomplished in this manner.

Campaign finance reform

Franklin Delano Roosevelt:

"We had to struggle with the old enemies of peace—business and financial monopoly, speculation, reckless banking, class antagonism, sectionalism, war profiteering. They had begun to consider the Government of the United States as a mere appendage to their own affairs. We know now that Government by organized money is just as dangerous as Government by organized mob. Never before in all our history have these forces been so united against one candidate as they stand today. They are unanimous in their hate for me—and I welcome their hatred."

Reverse Citizens United. Money is not speech. Corporations are not people. People are not animals. Abolish corporate personhood with federal and state constitutional amendments.

Mass incarceration/Drug War

End both mass incarceration and the Drug War which have gone beyond destabilizing neighborhoods to devastating entire cities and sometimes entire countries. Mass incarceration is slavery, as defined by the exception clause in the 13th Amendment.

Legalize marijuana. Decriminalize street drugs. Retrain police to protect, assist, and serve citizens rather than to hunt and kill citizens.

The Drug War cannot be won. The Drug War is already lost with no end in sight. The Drug War is a failed, out-dated policy from the 70s and 80s. Send the victims of this catastrophe of a War to drug treatment, mental therapy, and provide them with life skills training and a program of productive re-entry into society. Find better, more honorable priorities for police to fulfill.

Militarized police

Military weaponry should not be used on domestic soil against citizens of the United States. Citizens fund the police to protect and serve citizens, not to hunt and kill citizens. Community policing, as demonstrated by National Night Out, plus citizen governing boards provide the correct law enforcement balance to ensure fairness rather than terror as a criminal justice goal.

Civil Asset Forfeiture

Our police forces deserve better funding, better salaries, better benefits in equal proportion to the hazards they face on the job.

It is an absolute disgrace to send our police out into the communities in which they are expected to serve with a shopping list to make up for budget shortfalls by seizing citizens' assets. This is an embarrassment and a shame in a nation as wealthy as the United States. Our police should not have to create atmospheres of stress and tension just to gather up resources to pawn when the better solution is to actually pay these men and women what they are worth.

Equip our police with high quality gear *appropriate to the job*. Allow our police the benefit of a positive working environment and the hero status they deserve in the communities they serve.

For-profit money bail system

End this miserable, greedy industry under-written by predatory insurance corporations. The for-profit money bail system is a disgusting violation of the "innocent until proven guilty" expectation and is another corporate over-reach and tool of destructive economic injustice upon the lives of the poor and indigent.

Gun violence/Gun control

Congressman Joe Kennedy III:

"We can decide that one person's right to bear arms does not come at the expense of a neighbor's right to life, liberty and the pursuit of happiness."

The Second Amendment of the United States Constitution:

"A well regulated Militia, being necessary to the security of a free State, the right of the people to keep and bear Arms, shall not be infringed."

The Brady Bill requires background checks on individuals before the individual purchases a firearm from a federally-licensed dealer, manufacturer or importer. If there are no restrictions, ownership of the firearm may be transferred upon approval by the National Instant Criminal Background Check System (NICS) maintained by the FBI.

Some loopholes remain, for instance the gun show and online purchase loopholes that permits sale of weapons without background checks. Our U.S. Constitution is clear. Which means, we as a nation have failed our constitutional obligation to maintain a well-regulated militia. At this time, car ownership and liquor sales are more well-regulated than gun ownership.

Extend background checks to all private sales of firearms.

Electoral reform

Provide equal access of candidates to media, debate forums, voter information. Provide equal access of voters to candidate/ballot measure information and polling places.

The gold standard of elections is paper balloting, exit polling, hand-counting, automatic recounts of less than 1% difference.

End gerry-mandering. Stop fighting citizens on ranked choice or approval voting measures. Move election day to Saturday or Sunday. Reinstate the full force of the Voting Rights Act.

Immigration

Entrance and exit laws should be enforced equally rather than preference provided for certain groups from one country over another. Citizens of the nation are the priority.

Barbara Jordan:

"Deportation is crucial. Credibility in immigration policy can be summed up in one sentence: Those who should get in, get in; those who should be kept out, are kept out; and those who should not be here will be required to leave. The top priorities for detention and removal, of course, are criminal aliens. But for the system to be credible, people actually have to be deported at the end of the process."

And:

"It is both a right and a responsibility of a democratic society to manage immigration so that it serves the national interest."

And

"Our patience is growing thin toward those attempting to overwhelm the will of the American people by acts that

ignore, manipulate, or circumvent our immigration laws. Unless this country does a better job in curbing illegal immigration, we risk irreparably undermining our commitment to legal immigration."

And

"... a well-regulated system of legal immigration is in our national interest,"

And:

"Any nation worth its salt must control its borders."

Military intervention

James K. Galbraith:

"There is a reason for the vulnerability of empires. To maintain one against opposition requires war — steady, unrelenting, unending war. And war is ruinous — from a legal, moral and economic point of view. It can ruin the losers, such as Napoleonic France, or Imperial Germany in 1918. And it can ruin the victors, as it did the British and the Soviets in the 20th century. Conversely, Germany and Japan recovered well from World War II, in part because they were spared reparations and did not have to waste national treasure on defense in the aftermath of defeat... The real economic cost of Bush's empire building is twofold: It diverts attention from pressing economic problems at home and it sets the United States on a long-term imperial path that is economically ruinous."

Preferable to economically ruinous military interventions is a pivot towards diplomacy, international aid, plus cooperation with other nations in existing diplomatic bodies.

AUMF — Authorization for the Use of Military Force

The duty for declaration of war has been assigned by the U.S.

Constitution to the U.S. Congress. Not the U.S. President! The U.S. Congress has proven constitutionally derelict in taking responsibility for war power on behalf of the citizens they represent. The U.S. Congress has failed to check and balance the power of the U.S. President. This must change. The U.S. Congress must regain responsibility for war-making, or not war-making, and then provide accountability to the people of their districts for the reasons why or why not.

Defense spending

As pointed out by economist James K. Galbraith, the U.S. has over-extended its empire and is on a historical schedule of decline. Much as Rome, Spain, Portugal, France, England, Germany over-extended their military defense and then declined. The center cannot hold. Empire building abroad is destroying community building at home, also acknowledged by former president Dwight Eisenhower.

Defense spending is not just money allocated to the Department of Defense. This spending includes private military contractor CEO salaries, lobbyist salaries (to buy access to Congress), operation of military bases abroad, support personnel abroad, weapons development and testing, fossil fuel consumption, foreign aid, etc.

In 2011, a study by economists from the University of Massachusetts showed that putting this money used for "military defense" into any other area–infrastructure, transportation, alternative energy, health care, education– creates up to twice as many jobs as military spending does.

Close superfluous military bases abroad. It is time for our troops to return home. Support our troops! Stop abusing our troops! Bring our troops home where they belong to provide leadership in the retrofitting, rebuilding and revitalization of our damaged coastlines, cities, and suburbs. We need our troops and we need to pay them what they're worth!

Israel/Palestine

I support the work of Jews for Justice for Palestinians, an advocacy group in Great Britain, as well as Jewish Voice for Peace and If Not Now, advocacy groups in the United States. Peace, justice, and unity are the stated goals of these groups. Peace, justice, and unity are worthy goals of any nation, including the United States.

The United States has created more problems than it has solved in the Middle East overall, and has sacrificed too many lives of our U.S. military servicemen and women on ineffective Middle East strategies and endless war. Clearly, history has already proven that we are not the world's policeman.

The U.S. Congress should not be in the business of crafting unconstitutional legislation. Legislation that contradicts the First Amendment of the U.S. Constitution, including S-720 Israel Anti-Boycott Act, fits the definition of unconstitutional.

Alterations to our U.S. Constitution require a lengthy approval process. "A proposed amendment becomes part of the Constitution as soon as it is ratified by three-fourths of the States (38 of 50 States)." Alterations to our U.S. Constitution are not the provenance of any foreign power.

Foreign aid

Unless and until our citizens in the United States are fed, clothed, housed, educated, and provided with healthcare and basic income for a reasonably safe and secure existence, no foreign aid.

My Sweet Baby
[from *Tamerlane* (unpublished), 2019]

My DNA, my genes, my child
I will kill you or die trying
You came to me
With the metallic taste of poison

And inside me you grew
And grew and grew
My Sweet Baby
I will kill you very soon

No matter what they say
No matter how they complain
I've made the choice
I will kill you or die trying

You have no right to my body
Though you conceal yourself inside
Twisted, alien
Bent, aberrant; you are a monster

And so is your toxic father
You are mine, but you have no
Right to my life
Die, baby, die, right now, today

The Mountains Reach
[from *I Disappear: 3 Short Screenplays*, 2020]

Up to heaven, to the stars
To the universe
To join with God
To sing with the angels
We send our greetings to the world
We lift our Earth as a gift
To those who come to see
Our offerings
And hear
Our prayers
And not
Pass us by

Journey to Arusha

In Babylon, I worked as a mentor or peer counselor in the girls dormitory of a prestigious residential public school. My circumstances placed me in an interesting position during the launch of the coronavirus plandemic.

As news developed along the storylines practiced during Event 201, held in New York at Johns Hopkins University with participation from Bill and Melinda Gates, my school's administrators decided to send all students home. The final two months of the school year would be held online via various digital platforms.

While fortunate that I still had a job, because many did not, I did not enjoy interacting with the students on chat, videosharing, email, and the rest. The job I signed up for involved face to face human interaction and I missed that immediately. Even though I lived in isolated safety with security and janitorial staff, I disliked the silence of the empty school buildings with no students. Deer and other wildlife quickly overtook the school grounds because no kids were walking around or playing on the campus lawn.

Because of the plandemic, the boost in online technology consumerism meant that Big Tech became even bigger. While mom and pop, brick and mortar became smaller.

But as people quarantined and spent more time online, individual research into the origins of the plandemic was shared by billions of users. And soon, the amateur detectives who put the pieces together concluded that information about coronavirus did not add up to a whole.

During the last two weeks of March 2020, my own suspicions grew due to the numerous lies, contradictions, and medical gibberish about the virus reported by mainstream media. The overt mainstream media narrative, was consistently undermined by information revealed by billions of social media users. Most disturbing was the insistent rejection of natural remedies, immunity strengthening, sunshine, fresh air, exercise, and nutrition in favor of loud calls for worldwide mandatory vaccination, contact tracing, policing, surveillance.

However, suspicion quickly escalated to alarm by early April 2020 when the so-called health experts once again switched the narrative to declare that African Americans were now the face of coronavirus. However, I'd already examined those statistics and discovered that they also didn't add up to support the narrative. But soon, I noticed... that the statistics began to shift... to support the narrative! This is the same play book that Hitler used to turn the greater German population against the Jews, by referring to them as "syphillitic," thus encouraging Germans to decide the only way to save themselves from the public health emergency, was to get rid of the problem segment of the population.

According to the mainstream, Blacks who appeared healthy were actually asymptomatic carriers, disproportionately "at risk" of contaminating the larger population simply by leaving their homes and breathing air. And so the ugly, racist nature of North American society once again, as it always did, revealed itself underneath the same veneer of benevolence and concern that inspired medical experimentation during slavery, smallpox blankets, the Tuskeegee Experiment of injected syphyllis called medical treatment, the poisoning of hundreds in Guyana with sugary flavor-aid, Mississippi appendectomies, the spread of HIV via injections called smallpox vaccination, and the development of autism via injections also called vaccinations. And we learned online that Blacks in hospitals were being targeted and terminated to make the statistics support the narrative.

Months of quarantine and isolation in an empty residence hall meant that I had more time to read *Medical Apartheid* by Harriet Washington, *The Isis Papers* discussion on HIV/AIDs by Frances Cress Welsing, and the *Incredible Life of*

Henrietta Lacks by Rebecca Skloot. And the chilling end game became crystal clear. Africans and the African Diaspora were up for extermination and genocide by biological warfare. The greater US population was being brainwashed, like the Germans were brainwashed, into believing that preservation of their own lives depended upon our extermination.

More reading of documents created by so-called charities, think tanks, government bodies, and pharmaceutical companies revealed that the infrastructure for worldwide tracking and extermination of populations deemed "problematic" had been systematically laid and guided by doctors of the Jekyll, Frankenstein, Moreau, Lecter, Mengele, Kevorkian, Fauci variety. I felt sick inside when I remembered that I'd written an essay from nineteen years ago on this type of technology that I thought was too fantastic to believe. I even described such fears as "wacky." But it was not fantasy. It was history in the making!

And then... President John Pombe Magufuli of Tanzania, a doctorate in chemistry and mathematics exposed that the coronavirus test kits provided false positives. And we researchers learned that the test cycles were amplified higher than required to pick up stray viral remnants of previous vaccinations and infections. Meaning the number of cases were created with false data and that the reporting was "fake news." Numerous doctors, nurses, and morticians blew the whistle to reveal that they were pressured to report false cause of death and to commit insurance fraud.

More and more whistle-blowers came forward and some even revealed that patients did not die from coronavirus. Instead, the patients were killed by deliberate medical misdiagnosis and maltreatment. And the arrows continued to point towards Africans and the African Diaspora along with insistent whispers of contact, track, trace, isolate, quarantine... vaccination... for the greater good of society. Still, I kept myself busy by sewing masks out of old t-shirts and rigging up a face shield from half of a large-sized clear plastic juice bottle stapled to an elastic headband. Because I just wasn't sure.

At the same time, violence against African Americans, a pattern established in previous presidential election years escalated in 2020. Almost... as if... certain groups were working to provoke the rioting they failed to provoke during the 2016 presidential election cycle. The televised, ice-cold murder of George Floyd, preceded by the murders of Breonna Taylor, Ahmaud Arbery, Botham Jean, and so many others inflicted trauma, confusion, and anger on Africans and the African Diaspora. The excuse-making and refusal by Minneapolis law enforcement to arrest and detain Floyd's murderers seemed... deliberate acts to drive citizens waiting expectantly for justice to riot instead.

Meanwhile, local North American governments tightened restrictions on social movement, shut down businesses, and created economic fear, panic, and paranoia. And the powers that be said, unless you cooperate with our agenda, things will never get back to normal.

Meanwhile, Tanzania's president requested more frequent handwashing and temperature checks, but no forced wearing of masks and social distancing, testing, and/or quarantine. Being a Christian, he also requested prayer.

Another African nation, Madagascar, created an organic cure with the main ingredient announced as artemisia, which was soundly ridiculed and rejected as dangerous though artemisia has been used for treatment since biblical times. Similar to the rejection of hydroxychloroquine as a treatment, though HCQ and quinine had been safely used as a preventative for a variety of viral, bacterial, and painful conditions for centuries. Many natural remedies including intravenous vitamin C and food-grade hydrogen peroxide were also put into the dangerous quackery categories, along with other medical treatments such as alpha interferon, apirivine, remdesvir, ivermectin.

Mainstream media continued to insist that increased policing, surveillance, contact tracing, tracking, quarantine, isolation, and lockdown of jobs, businesses, and the economy were the only treatments for coronavirus. And the main targets continued to focus on Africans and the African Diaspora as problematic. And gleeful anticipation of the decimation of these groups seemed to be spoken of repeatedly.

And then suddenly, Tanzania announced that it would accept international flights and allow visitors, with no requirement other than handwashing and temperature checks. And I thanked my lucky stars that I hoarded my paychecks rather than spend them. And that I kept a current passport whether or not I traveled. And that I had a safe place to store my belongings. I had more than I realized.

I quietly purchased a round trip ticket and began packing. Every once in a while, I carried a larger than normal-sized garbage bag to the trash dumpster so that I wouldn't alert security and janitorial staff that I was about to make a move. I couldn't risk contact tracing that might result in me not being allowed to board a flight out of the country.

A moment of panic came when the airline cancelled the flight and refused to refund, instead offering me a credit at a later date. Many phone calls later, I secured the refund. In the meantime, I had many discussions with family members who expressed concern for my safety for my trip to Africa.

Throughout May, I worked cleaning the empty rooms at the residence hall, interacted with the students online, and tried to find some measure of normalcy in troubling times. Cities were on fire across North America as protestors and rioters gathered in the streets. A part of me wondered if the protestors and rioters were simply desperate to get out of their homes and gather with others in response to the lockdowns and isolation. They were willing to march together for miles just for the opportunity to exercise and socialize with others and breath fresh air and feel sunshine.

I purchased another flight, then cancelled it myself after being talked out of it by one family member. Then finally, with all questions answered and issues settled, I purchased another round trip flight. More cancellations, and at least one attempt to double-charge, which meant more phone calls to travel agents as I continued to try to find a way out of the country and protect my bank account at the same time.

I sent copies of my identity documents to family members, and one family member received a copy of my will. That person said that they understood why I did so.

With everything in order that I could put in order, I quit my job as a residential mentor and peer counselor the same day I moved out of the dormitory. I dropped some extra clothes and shoes off at a church. I rented a U-haul and drove everything I couldn't fit into my suitcase, backpack, and purse to my family home. I returned the U-haul, finished cleaning my apartment in the empty dormitory. During the drive to the airport, I noticed that my night vision had sharpened, likely because of the vitamin cocktails I'd been taking since March.

But when I attempted to fly out, the agent claimed I arrived too late to get through security. So I rebooked another flight. I repacked my suitcase and picked up an extra key to my car because I would store it my cousin's house rather than sell it. Because I just didn't know how the story would end.

On my next attempt to fly out, I got lost on the way to airport. And once again, the agent claimed that I arrived too late to get through security. So I rebooked, again. And then I picked up a laptop, and removed more heavy items from my suitcase to get the weight down because I was now carrying a laptop.

The third time was the charm! I arrived on time, but the agent was still rude and impatient, and seemingly unaware of how to process passports for international flights. But after a long phone consultation, the agent processed my paperwork, I got through security, I got on the flight. I wore a face mask and face shield that I acquired from an Army outlet store.

First leg of domestic flight, no problem. Middle seat empty. Second leg of domestic flight, no problem. Middle seat empty. Third leg of the flight was from Washington DC to Frankfurt, Germany. Here there was a problem. The gate agents claimed that Frankfurt's airport would not allow me to connect because of rising cases in the United States.

I decided that I would wait it out. I would outlast the gate agents. I would stand at the counter, and look at them. I had all day and all night to just look at them and I would do that all day and all night until they put me on a flight. Because I had nothing at all planned for the rest of the day except flying out of the country so I had all day and all night. And I had nothing left to return to anyway, no job, no apartment, no car, no belongings. All in storage or shut down. Not causing problems or saying a word at the gate, just looking at the agents, even willing to wait for the second shift. After a long discussion, several phone calls, and me just basically standing there staring, I was allowed to board the flight to Frankfurt.

On this flight, the two middle seats were empty. I'd never flown across the ocean. Thankfully, there was enough time on the flight for me to watch three movies and I could forget that the plane was travelling over a vast amount of water. In fact, I could have stretched out on my empty row and gone to sleep, but someone invited himself to sit on the end of my row. I had two really good meals and a snack. Towards the end of the flight to Frankfurt, the airline requested a contact trace form, which I had already researched to discover was not for the airport or the German government, but for a random private health clinic in Ohio... not official. And so I treated the request with the exact amount of respect it deserved.

I used Frankfurt airport's wifi to email an update to my family and update my laptop's computer settings, but I eventually ran low on battery. The gift shop in the airport did not have an electrical adapter for US electronics. The store had all other adapters, but not US. I suspected this meant something, but wasn't sure what.

Once again, I got the dreaded flight cancellation email for the fourth leg to Addis Ababa, which the travel agent booked to overlap with third leg, the flight to Frankfurt. I called the travel agent once again, but I couldn't explain the situation clearly because I was exhausted and confused about what time zone I was in. The travel agent told me to contact the airline directly.

So I went to airline ticket counter to get boarding passes for the fourth and fifth leg of flights, fully prepared to stare and look with sadness, but there was no problem. I boarded the flight and it seemed like the plane was only one-third full of mostly Arabs, Indians, and Africans, and I believe I was the sole American. I hoped they were also transporting cargo to make up the financial shortfall.

And then, I finally did it! I arrived on the Continent of my ancestors. Addis Abbaba, Ethiopia was the fourth leg. And then I flew into Dar es Salaam on a half-full plane on the fifth and final leg, this time mostly Africans. I made it to Tanzania!

I carried my own digital thermometer so I already knew I would pass the temperature check. I filled out the Ebola contact trace form, had my passport verified, made visa payment, passed the duty station with nothing to declare. And then I threw away my mask, per the sign at the airport. No masks! No social distancing! Fresh air! A real society.

And the very first thing I chose to do in the land of my ancestors was argue with the taxi driver over fare to the bus station. I arrived too late to get the bus to Arusha, I would have to spend the night in Dar es Salaam. So I decided to eat a meal with the taxi driver (fish, fries, beans, rice, salad, watermelon), who was now my only friend in Africa. Then he arranged my hotel room, carried my luggage, told me how to get bus the to Arusha, and arranged my transportation to the bus station the next morning.

Africa!

I spent my first night in Dar es Salaam huddled under the covers in my hotel room, covered in frankincense essential oil to keep the mosquitoes away. And I listened to the street action that carried on from night to morning without stop.

The front desk wakes me and I'm still trying to figure out the plumbing in the bathroom but somehow, I make it work. It's dark thirty in the morning en route to the bus station. It's crazy! It's zany! So many people! I'm over-whelmed, until I focus on the fact that I'd traveled south of the border to Mexico City and Havana. I'd been in the Third World before, not on this level, but close. I survived the experience, and it was that experience I should draw upon for reference whenever I panicked.

There's no such thing as social distancing on this bus to Arusha. I cannot wear a face mask or face shield because it is too hot. Plus, no one else is wearing personal protective equipment, me doing so would identify me as a foreignor and make me a target. So I breathe in the air that everyone breathes out and hope that the zinc, quercetin, and multi-vitamin cocktails I'd taken since March would protect me. And I see that there are also elderly men and women on the bus who don't seem to have any of the problems the media declared that they would. No one is convulsing or frothing at the mouth with coronavirus.

Tanzanians benefit from strong, protective, nationalistic leadership. President John Pombe Magufuli said "enough!" to the coronavirus campaign which seemed to cause anger, stress, fear, and resentment in the population. He said Tanzania survived HIV, malaria, and Ebola, the nation will also survive coronavirus. He told the people to continue to believe in God, work, socialize, interact, produce, go outdoors, exercise, get sunshine, eat well, rely on natural remedies, and no wearing of face masks. There are temperature checks and required handwashing, but no face masks and no social distancing. No contact tracing and no tracking.

From what I see, people are not dropping dead in the streets or suffering. I came to Tanzania specifically so I wouldn't have to wear a face mask, be forced to social distance, and then walk and live in fear and suspicion and resentment of others. I didn't want to live like that because that's how people in the States live which is the reason I left.

Also, we are not meant to re-breathe our own carbon dioxide, which is a waste product. That's like drinking your own blood or urine or sweat. Eating your own feces and dried nose mucus. It's just not meant to be done. You could probably survive the first few times, but after long term consumption of your own body waste, you're gonna have problems.

So, I decide that I will live free, happy, and healthy in Tanzania.

Though the bus is called a safari bus, I laugh to myself because none of us have any intention of going on safari. We're regular folks trying to get home. However, I look at the countryside as we pass through trying to figure out what's going on here. Many banana and citrus trees. An amazing amount of corn that I didn't expect.

I watch with worry as the windows open, then close, then open, then close. And then I worry that none of the towns have identifying signs. And neither do the streets have signs. Ummm... where am I? How can I ask? The only Kiswahili I know is hakuna matata from *The Lion King*. Even if I asked, it seems like no one could tell me the answer, because they're all speaking Kiswahili. As we arrive to each town where the bus stops, I say Arusha (?) to my seatmate. But she says no. And then she gets off the bus and I have no one to ask where I am.

I decide that I will disembark where the most amount of people disembark. That's the only logic I could come up with. And so... I exit the bus with the biggest crowd.

Arusha!

I arrive at dark thirty at night. And take the taxi from the bus station to the airbnb. A whole entire three blocks. I feel silly, but I go ahead and pay the guy. There was a night watchman, lots of iron bars and locks on the door. The host greeted me and showed me around, plus a place nearby to eat.

And I collapsed into bed.

Soon, I would find other members of the Diaspora tribe. I would know my way around sufficiently that I could be of service to other disoriented new arrivals and help them to adjust.

My traumatic stress would lessen in an environment where most people looked like me. I could release the pain and anger of racism for every day I lived in North America. I could contribute to my new community by teaching English, history, civics, geography, gardening. I could edit English language publications. I could give and not just take. I could defy the stereotypes and lies spoken about Black Americans by being the best Black American role model possible. I could blend into the population, learn the language, the dress code, the culture and customs, how to conduct business.

I would not regard my mistakes and errors as negatives. Every day would bring a new adventure and a learning experience that wouuld help me grow stronger.

I would be no longer an African in America.

I would become an African in Africa!

My Personal Experience as a Teacher
[Summative Essay for TESOL Certification, 2020]

English classes usually provided my highest scores during junior high and high school. For this reason, I have served as a reading tutor and English spoken language tutor since the undergraduate college years and graduate school.

As an undergraduate, I volunteered at the local public library in the U.S. to read to children ages seven, eight, nine, ten. I read age-appropriate materials to individual children, or read to them in groups as part of the library's after-school program. In this instance, the students were already English speakers, but emotional support, role modeling, and keeping the children focused on positive activities also played a big part of the programming.

As a graduate student of library science, I taught bibliographic instruction to undergraduate students of a university that was rapidly moving towards online technology. This meant that I introduced students to basic computer usage as well as how to seek information via online databases.

After graduate school, I worked as a professional librarian teaching similar bibliographic and technology courses as a reference librarian in an academic library. This was a cooperative effort with professors to ensure that their students could maintain the rapid pace of research requirements. While some library courses I taught were generally unspecific and voluntary, many courses were at the specific request of instructors, which altered motivation, but ended with similar goals of research adeptness from the students.

I have had the benefit of not only teaching in academic libraries, but also in public schools as a substitute teacher.

Based upon my background of political science and library science, I had the flexibility of teaching English classes, history, social science, civics, home economics, and a few other vocational classes. It did quickly appear to me that the motivations and attitudes of the students seemed more positive in the vocational classes, which the students chose to attend. With the English classes, I had to work harder to encourage the cooperation of the students who were not attending these classes by their own choice, rather by school requirement.

Besides classroom teaching, I also volunteered as a voice-over artist to read and record English language books for blind and dyslexic students. This training also helped me to pay attention to how I use my voice to translate emotions and feelings, as well as pitch, clarity, pace, and volume.

Finally, I participated as a residential mentor for a prestigious high school where my instruction was more informal, providing emotional support and social activities within a dormitory setting. Once again, I learned many types of fun activities and exercises from fellow staff and the students themselves to hold their attention, keep them engaged and focused, as well as helping them with life and interpersonal skills.

The majority of my teaching has been with students of high school age, university level, and adult learners on a variety of subjects. However, at the moment, I've find myself teaching English to one set of younger students ages five, six, seven, eight. The other set of students are teenagers ages fourteen, fifteen, sixteen. Their first language is Kiswahili.

While before I was on the periphery of most classrooms, with these students, I am the main instructor which means I evaluate their language levels, their motivations and goals. I select course text books, supporting materials, real media, authentic and authentic materials, classroom curriculum. I pay attention to language level and cultural appropriateness, ensuring that they understand the variations between American and British English. I balance reading, writing, listening, speaking and attempt to ensure a variety of experiences, within a standard framework so they know what the expectations are.

The TESOL coursework has been tremendously helpful in providing ideas, suggestions, guidance, and many examples and recommendations of how to make learning easier and better, and how to manage the classroom for the very best results. The intelligence, hard work, and positivity of the students has also been helpful to my growth as an English instructor. While I had previous experience teaching in a classroom setting and with individual students, I knew I had much more to learn, and taking the TESOL course while teaching in real life made the learning immediately gratifying since I could see the results in real time.

For the teenage students, ensuring that English and not Kiswahili was spoken in the classroom was a challenge, but not as much a challenge for the younger students. Fortunately, I was able to use some of the classroom warm up games to encourage more English, as well as the recommendations on classroom management. On one occasion, due to circumstances, the younger students joined the older students in the classroom. I immediately deputized the older students to tutor the younger students in reading. I am also very quick to make sure the students know that English class is a safe zone where they can practice English skills and not fear any mockery for mistakes.

Overall, I have found that games and competitions increase excitement and learning, but we also conduct drills, and I ask the students specific questions so they can feel proud of the knowledge they've acquired. I've found that the more the students hear themselves and others increasing their knowledge and experience with English, the more their own comfort levels and confidence increase.

This TESOL course has reminded me of how complicated and complex the English language is and how native speakers might take the language ability for granted. Teaching English to non-native speakers quickly clarifies many questions, and teaching English as a second language has also served to remind me of how far the students I work with have already come.

In fact, while they have been learning Kiswahili to English skills, I am fortunate to have also learned English to Kiswahili skills. I can say that one important aspect of a teacher of English to non-native speakers is that there is still much to learn, especially if a teacher is sometimes willing to become a student.

Riding the Piki Piki

The second morning of my new life in Tanzania, I awaken with a list of activities for myself to accomplish. Not safari, not a museum, not exploring a traditional village, instead errands! Find an ATM, an electrical adapter, wifi, photo film developer, mundane, everyday things like this.

But as I explore my new community in downtown Arusha on a mini walking tour, I can't help but notice a lot of men sitting on motorcycles gazing upon me with hunger and need in their eyes. I mean, I'm flattered, I guess. I did take time with my appearance and everything, after all. And as I draw nearer to the wolf pack while I'm trying to find my destinations, the whispers and catcalls begin.

"Hey mommy! Where you going? You want to ride on my piki piki? Mommy! Come with me. Ride with me. Ride my piki piki."

And I gasp from the forwardness of their blatant invitations. I mean, I've been in large cities like Chicago, Houston, Dallas, New Orleans, Havana, even Mexico City. And I've heard catcalls before, but never on this level. Also, I was given reason to understand that Tanzania was a conservative Christian and Muslim nation. But on my very first day, groups of men that I don't even know continue to ask me to ride their piki pikis.

I feel extremely insulted because I'm sure the American rap videos exported around the world have led men to think American women go around grinding and riding on anything they can lift their leg against. But this ain't that, okay?

I try common street tactics like no eye contact, frowning, glaring, crossing the street. But the cat calls continue and there are even more motorcycle wolf packs.

And then I get angry.

And so, I say to one, "Sir! I don't even know who you are for you to ask me to ride your... piki piki. Don't talk to me like that."

Because while I am out walking the streets, I am most certainly not a streetwalker. I work, but I am not a working girl. I'm a professional, but not a professional. I am hustling along, but I am not on the hustle. Surely, they know the difference?

But the blatant requests persist and now I look at my outfit. I'm wearing pants all the way down to my ankles and a long sleeve shirt to my wrists covered by a denim jacket. My backpack hides everything else. What is setting them off?

And now, even more men are hanging out of minibuses making similar comments, this time in Kiswahili, so I can only guess that I'm receiving similar insults. And I just can't figure out why they are grinning so wide and staring at me with such eagerness and waving their hands at me with come hither gestures. I don't even know them and I just feel they're being way too forward with the flirting. I wonder about the lack of common decency and respect and decorum because now I feel attacked.

I'm sure they've all figured out that I'm American, likely single because no man is escorting me, and maybe I'm willing to accept any and all who ask me to ride their piki pikis.

Now, I could have solved this riddle any number of ways. For instance, this could have happened.:

I look around for a police officer, and I finally see one. And as I approach, the wild invitations continue. And I wait for the police officer to reprimand those men because he can hear them too, but he says nothing. He's actually waiting for me to speak, with a casual stance, and a look of inquiry while catcalls continue to rain down in front of us both.

Finally, I ask the police officer in a voice that shakes, "Why do they talk to me like that?"

He cocks his head to the side.

"Is it because I'm a woman from America?"

And suddenly, the police officer looks interested. "Oh, you're an American?"

"Yes!" I tell him. And I wave towards the traffic. "They've been yelling at me all morning."

And I wait expectantly for justice. At least a lecture from him to those men on how to treat women they don't know and have never met with respect.

And that's when I have not only the concepts of piki piki, but also dala dala explained to me while the police officer laughs for an extra long time afterward.

And as the officer throws his head back for another round of laughing, I feel like he's doing way too much. My face is brown, of course, but I can feel it turning a little red. Because I feel silly. And also ashamed. And also rather vain. And extremely Western in my mindset, like a Karen. And I'm just not used to feeling this way.

But fortunately, dear reader, I'm relieved to say all that did not happen. I do not solve the riddle the Karen way. I solve it by close observation until I figure it out:

Like I mentioned, I've been in large cities and I've been catcalled. But I saw none of what I just experienced explained on the websites and blogs I researched prior to arrival. Like the Matrix, some things cannot be explained, you just have to experience it for yourself.

As I walk the streets of Arusha, not as a streetwalker, but as a pedestrian, I can't help but notice that the same eager offers to ride piki piki get issued to elderly men and women, anyone and everyone walking, in fact. First, the offer. Second, haggle over price. Third, away they go!

The motorcycle taxi drivers and minibus wranglers were offering me tickets to ride to a destination, and nothing else other than that. Plus, I would pay them for the ride, they wouldn't pay me.

They are small business owners, working hard, and they are professionals, just like me.

I have to be honest, a small part of me is now hurt. After all,

I did take care with my appearance this morning. I can only hope that the piki piki drivers forgive and forget my mistake as time passes.

Anyone and everyone can ride the piki piki. I've ridden many times now and enjoyed myself greatly.

I do have my favorites though. They know who they are. And they are very forgiving.

The Lion Roars

When the lion roars, I do not feel afraid
I love to see his beautiful leonine face
The eyes like jewels
The teeth that gleam white
The skin that glows and draws me near

Every time the lion sees me, he roars
He laughs, and I laugh with the lion
I never run away
Only towards the lion
And he laughs and roars louder

The Sun Shines

The blaze and the glow and the heat
The joy this gift brings
Life, health, strength

We, who love you
Your children that you raise
Lift our hands up

We dance and play and revel
Because you endure
Before us, with us, after us

How wonderful you make the world
Highly wanted and
Highly desired

Stay with us
We need you
The sun shines

White, yellow, orange
Tangerine, peach dreams
The greatest gift of life

The People Live

The death-bringer fails
The people live
Everything you take
The world will give

Stronger than you
Evil disappears
Happier than you
Despite your sneers

What made this beast
Wicked, so monstrous
A pathetic loser
That no one could trust

We know the darkness
Hidden under the smile
The simple inch we gave
You turned into a mile

Not fit for humans
The animals won't have you
Repulsive to all
Can't walk down an avenue

The lair you tricked out
Is your prison cell
Your hollow corpse
Alien indwelt

You are not one of us
We all know it
The people live
The alien doesn't

Damaged, But We Still Love You

When you gave us to them
For mirrors and beads and pieces of silver
You killed us both
Because we were always
Stronger together than apart
Some of you kept the
Generational wealth you earned
As slavers
Of different tribes
And to this day, you still
Make excuses
You smile and laugh
And you cannot understand
Why we do not laugh with you
You tell us to call you
Mama, Papa, Sister, Brother
But Mama, Papa, Sister, Brother
Would not do such things
Would not say such things
You call us guests
You call us tourists
And visitors and foreign
You call us strangers, even as you
Reach your hand into our pockets
We tell you what happened to us
After they took us

After they took everything from us
After they held guns and whips and knives
At our throats and dared us to
Speak our African language
Practice our African culture
Worship our African gods
Use our African names
Remember our African traditions
Remember our African ways
They promised a real death
Not just the living death of
A brainwashed zombie who
Performs for the master's delight
And delivers children for the master
To sell and build wealth for the master
The daily torture of the enslaved
The trauma and mental stress of
Constant hatred with no escape
The raped, abused, traumatized, tortured
Ones who managed to survive
And maintain some semblance of sanity
You look into their eyes
As they tell you their story
Of what happened after they took
Everything, including children
People that we loved and adored
People who made the living
Bearable
After they took everything we
Loved and believed in
You look, and you say
It's not so bad

You look, and you say
That was a long time ago
You look, and you say
You complain too much
You look, and you say
Work harder
Stop expecting
Stop talking
That language
We do not want to hear
Your words
Unless and until
You speak the way
That we will hear you
Speak our African language
Practice our African culture
Worship our African gods
Use our African names
Remember our African traditions
Remember our African ways
And forget
The four hundred years
It took you to develop a
New culture, tradition, history, religion
In order to survive
We tell you what happened to us yesterday
What happens to us today
What will happen to us tomorrow
The torture that remains
A part of our life every day
And still and still and still
You smile and laugh and say

Forget, forget all of that
Forget every last bit of that
Once more a brainwashing
Relinquish your identity once more
The four hundred years of your
Culture that you developed has
No place among us here
We do not accept the mutation
That you have now become
That they made you
Fix yourselves
Or else
Remain a stranger
In a strange land
A guest
A tourist
A visitor
A foreignor
An aberration
All we want from you
Is the wealth that you used
To relinquish to your master
That, we will accept
That and only that can belong to us
And then you may leave
The same way you came
As strangers

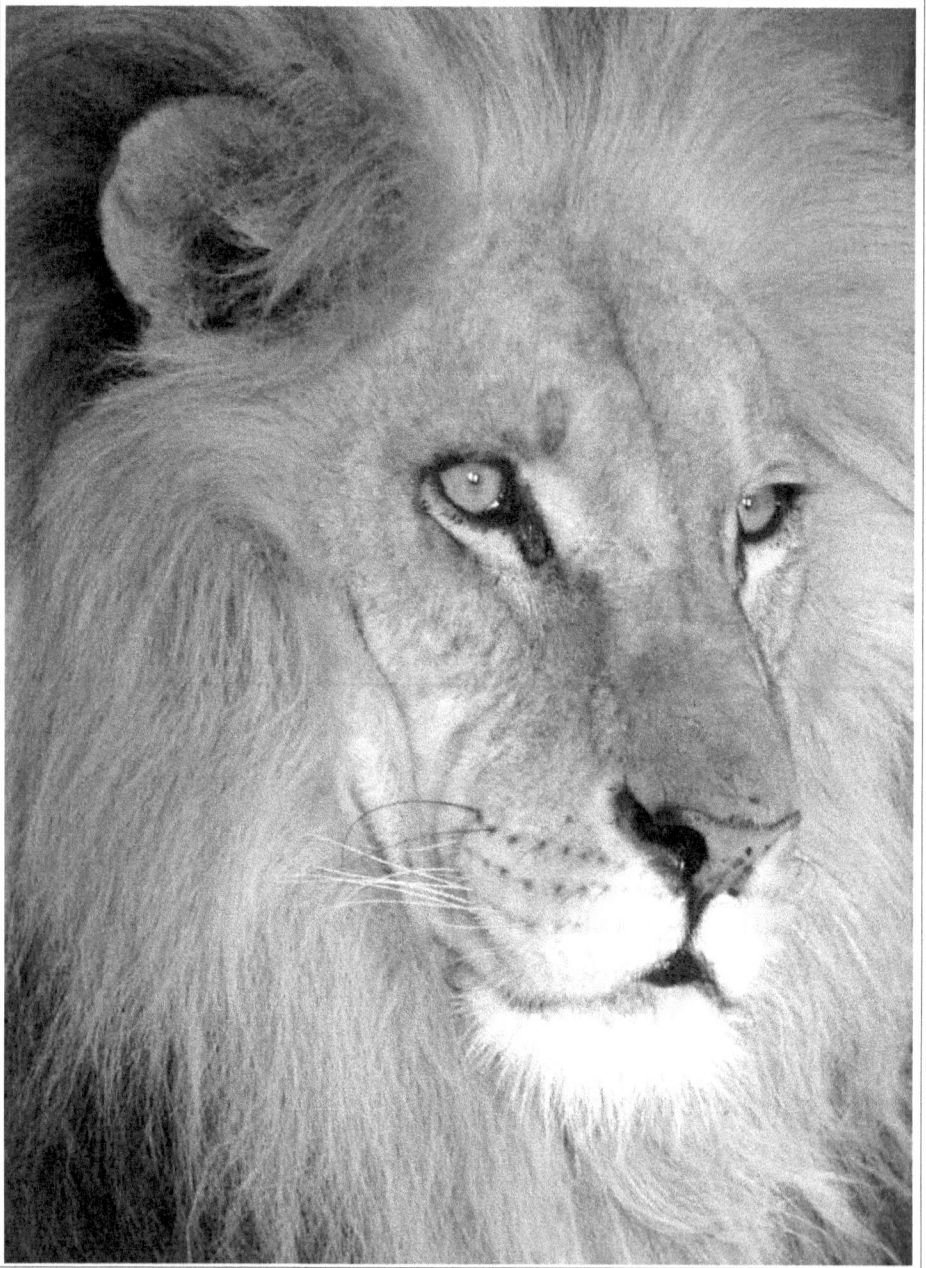

"Darica Lion 07168." Nevit Dilmen. Wikipedia Commons. 2007.

On a rooftop in Arusha with the Diaspora Tribe.

The Diaspora Tribe continues to grow
and expand across Africa.

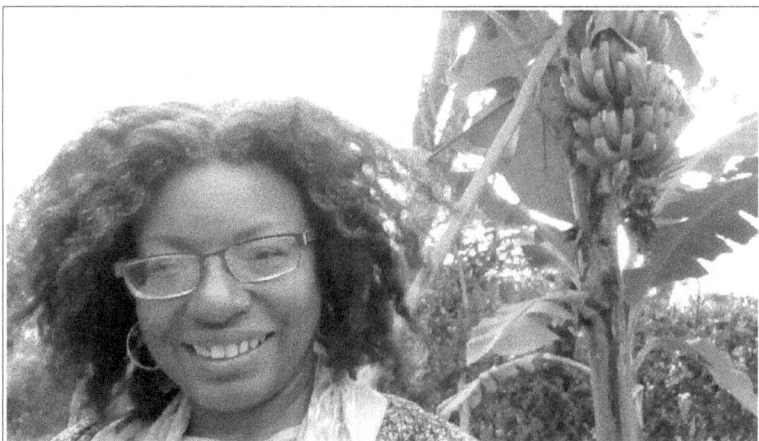

Face-to-face with tropicals like papaya, mango, guava, banana, sugarcane, cassava!

A papaya tree and a clothesline take advantage of the abundant solar energy.

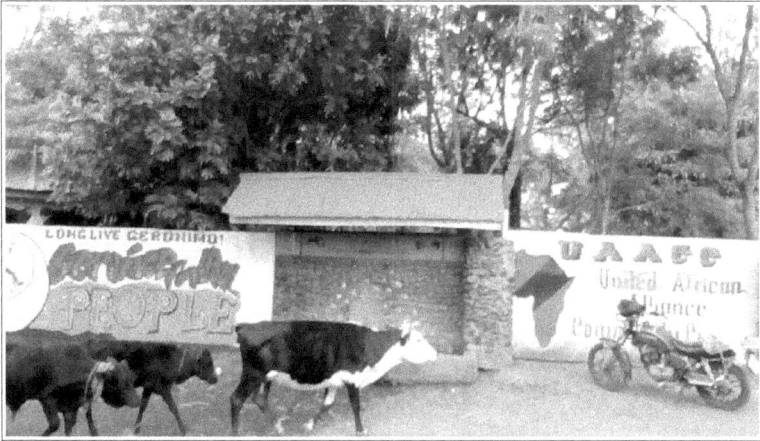

Thank you to Pete and Charlotte O'Neal for establishing a legacy of community service in Tanzania and beyond.

Rural road and path in Imbaseni Village.

The volcanic soil results in strong, sturdy, dark green crops that do not require fertilizer, herbicides, or insecticides.

Mount Meru overlooks the Arusha region.

Private English school in Maji ya Chai

I am satisfied with my choices.

About the Author

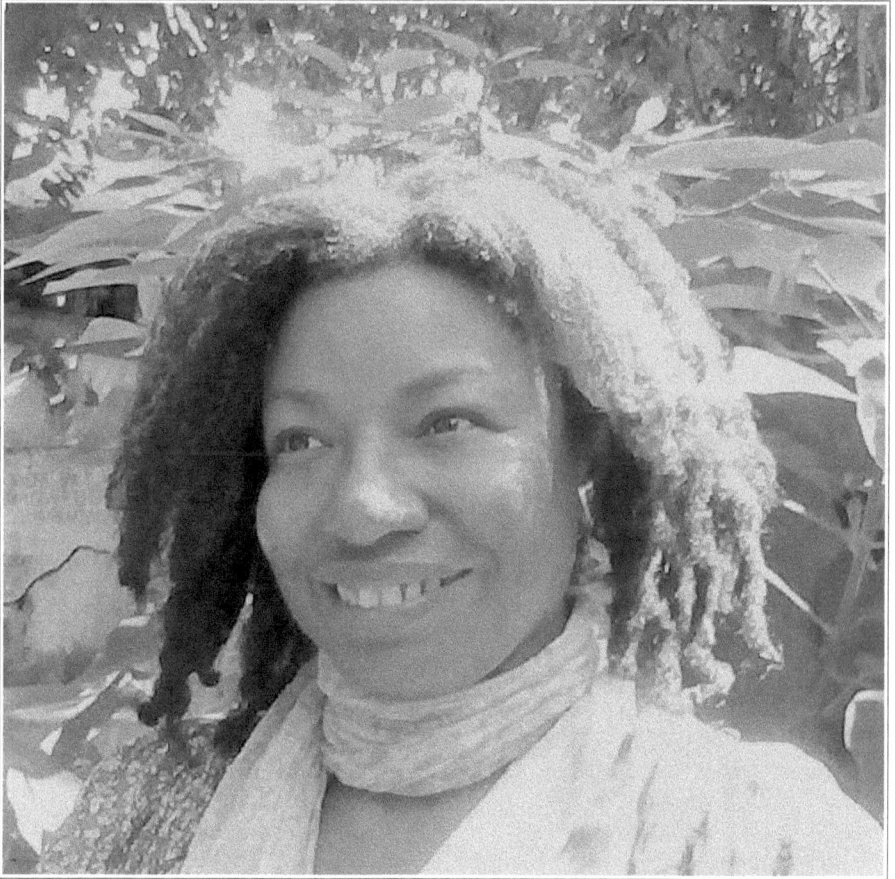

Lee McQueen enjoys writing, research, water colors, gardening, and traveling. She has been a librarian, a bookstore owner, and a substitute teacher and holds an MLS from SUNY-Buffalo, a BA from Xavier University, and coursework in public affairs at the University of Texas at Austin. Now editor and publisher at McQueen Press, her projects include novels, poetry, short stories, screenplays, and greeting cards.

Author's Note

After the events of September 11, 2001, North America experienced a rapid shift away from civil liberties and individual privacy towards heightened domestic surveillance and the concept of "pre-emptive strike," as a new national defense strategies. Though promised as temporary measures, these violations of personal freedom and common decency became the new normal.

Although it took too many years, a majority of North Americans now understand how physically, psychologically, morally, spiritually, economically damaging, unjustified, and misguided those actions were. All those who cheered for and participated in retaliation and destruction will have to continue to live with themselves for what they have done.

"The Ship of Fools" describes a world in which humans are treated like animals, captured by higher intelligence and forced to breed in unspeakable ways for eventual harvesting of their bodies. Everything that happens in the poem to the humans on an alien planet, already happens to cattle animals here on Earth. "My Sweet Baby" is about disease, not pregnancy.

When I wrote about Digital Angel in 2001, such track and trace devices were the speculative mainstays of science fiction and fantasy. Cell phones were not ubiquitous then. Even I, the writer, described the mere suggestion as "wacky." Such rumor-mongering developed on the wilder side of the Internet, the places where accusations of alien beings among us on Earth also resided.

However, only a few years later, the common cell and smartphones would come to perform much of what Digital Angel envisioned. The Lucifrase Quantum Dot Tattoo has now arrived to wide acclaim by mainstream media in 2020 with the support of medical, legal, and technology industries, plus governments around the world. This new technology fills in what gaps of freedom and privacy remain, thus completing the destruction of mind, body, soul, and spirit.

Acknowledgments

Thank you to the people who have supported my writing career throughout the years, most especially my family, the McQueens. I have a strong belief in the power of community and I readily admit that I did not "make it on my own."

My family, babysitters, teachers, professors, friends, heroes, acquaintances, and sometimes random passersby had something to do with the results you, the reader, see before you.

We humans are social creatures, not islands. Even the loners and introverts cannot survive inside a vacuum with their sanity intact.

The world is a better place when we live and thrive in harmony. Thank you to those who made my world a better place to live.

ISBN-13: 978-1-7352369-0-2
Short Screenplay Collection
2020

These screenplays examine the moral depths and horror that extreme income inequality and deprivation would drive people to explore. Horror fills the lives of those forced into a corner by systematic, destructive greed. These are the people who have to decide which child can eat dinner tonight and which child has to wait until breakfast tomorrow. They sell everything they own until there is nothing remaining to sell but themselves. Open this book, if you dare, visualize the degradation that unrestrained and unregulated capitalism visit upon 99% of the population. Feel something, even if it is to be driven insane, and know that you too are human and that what happens to the characters in these stories can also happen to you.

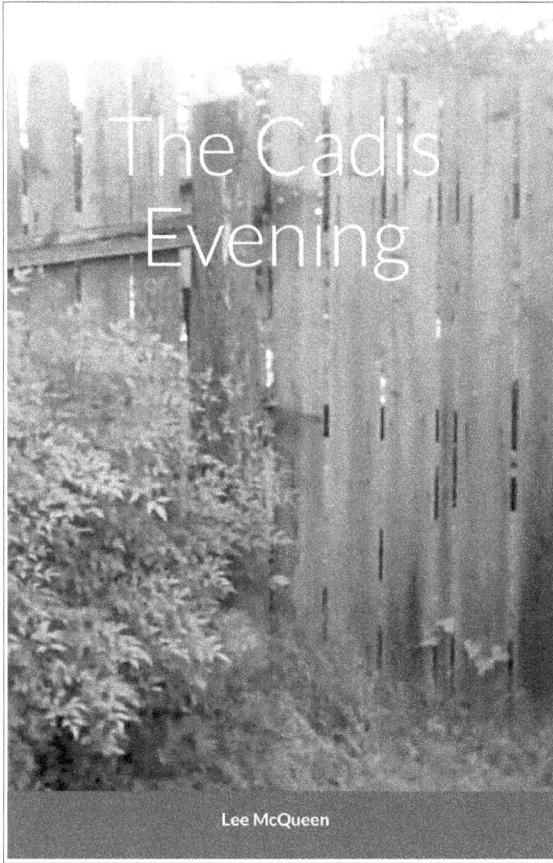

The Cadis Evening

Lee McQueen

ISBN-13: 978-1-7352369-1-9

2020 2nd ed

Stephanie Madison, a pariah to her family, launches a successful suicide attack against her employer, Cadis Industries. Though Stephanie dies in the attack, the strange menace that stalked Stephanie's life now targets her niece, Marietta Brazil. Forced to flee her city of birth as well as her adopted home, Marietta finally draws a line in the sand to confront the corrupt forces that destroyed her family. But though she fights the evil outside, can she truly face the darkness within?

The Dark Fantastic
Lee McQueen

Short Screenplay Collection
ISBN-13: 978-0-9798515-5-1
2013
These screen-ready tales of dark fantasy, horror, and adventure reflect possible rather than impossible worlds. Great stories for lovers of afro-futurism and speculative fiction. Plenty of monologues and dialogues for drama students and teachers, actors, screenwriters, producers, and directors.

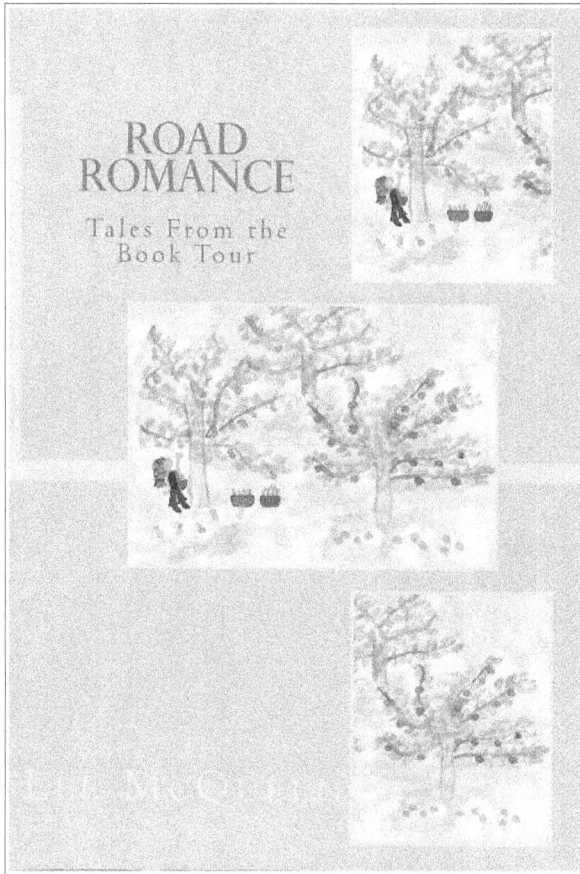

Travel Memoir

ISBN-13: 978-0979851568

2013

In 2012, Lee McQueen traveled from Colorado through Kansas, Oklahoma, Arkansas, Tennessee, Mississippi, Alabama, Georgia, Missouri, Illinois, Iowa, Nebraska, and then back to Colorado to promote her latest romance novel. From Beale Street to Route 66 to the Great River Road, to Colfax Avenue--in the spirit of Jack Kerouac and Johnny Appleseed--she fell in love with the road. This collection of journal entries, blog postings, narration in retrospect, and watercolors reveals surprises on Lee's journey through Middle America.

Suspense/Romance Novel
ISBN-13: 978-0979851575
2012
A cross-country chase carries Tolly Henry and Scott Windrunner on an adventure from Midwestern rolling prairies to southwestern Rocky Mountains. Roadside motels, truck stops, corn silos, and windmills guide Scott's whirlwind rundown of Tolly amid echoes of past military service, domestic violence, and post-traumatic stress.

Action/Adventure Screenplay

ISBN-13:978-0979851599

2nd ed.

2011

On a Christian mission to redeem slaves in Sudan, a reformed female gang member Davey is kidnapped and sold into slavery herself. She uses her former street experiences and talent for leadership to convince the other slaves to break free and flee to the Ethiopian border. Everything Davey has ever learned will save her life.

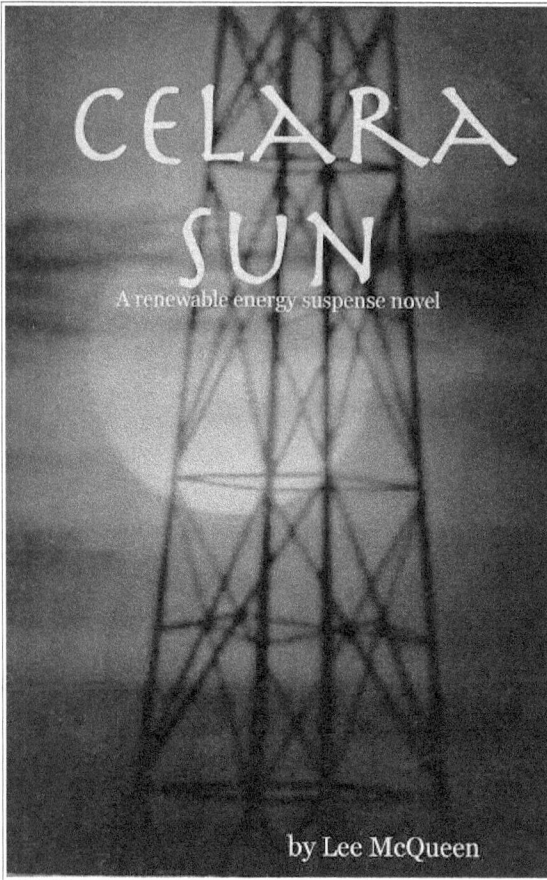

Suspense/Drama Novel
ISBN-13: 978-0979851582
2010

As *Dallas* and *Dynasty* showcased the wealth, sex, intrigue, and power that drove the oil industry, so *Celara Sun* reveals the tumultuous world behind solar and wind. Martina Butler matches Alexander King step-for-step in a battle of wills to control Lake City's solar and wind energy markets. During the green revolution, the players realize that life moves forward, never backward—and it certainly doesn't stand still.

Writer in the Library!

41 Writers Reveal How They Use Libraries to Develop Their Skill, Craft & Careers

by
Lee McQueen

Non-fiction/Reference
ISBN-13: 978-0979851544
2008

This non-fiction reference work collects the interviews and submissions of fiction and non-fiction writers who discuss the impact of libraries on their career development. Numerous transcripts, photos, biographies, library quotations, footnotes, a glossary, and an index present the information as a teaching tool for the reader.

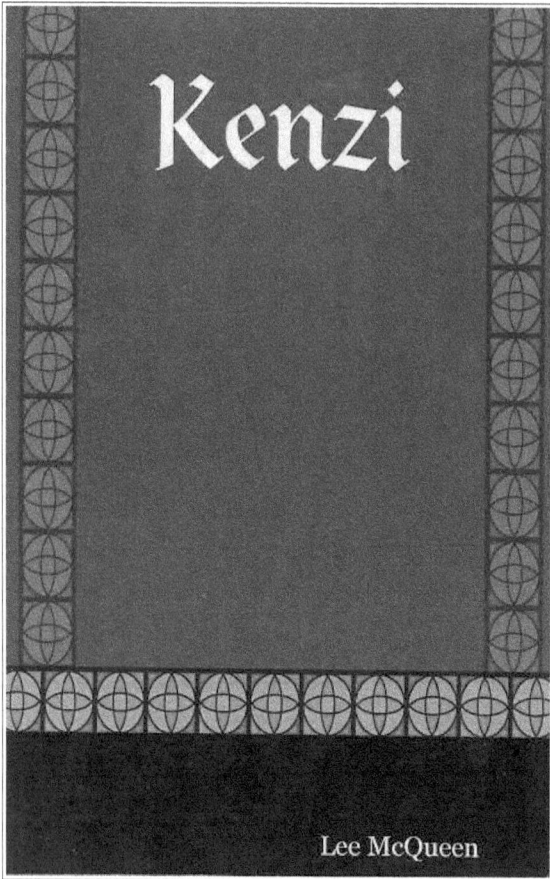

Romance/Family Drama Novel
ISBN-13: 978-0979851520
2007
Kenzi, an intelligent, sensitive woman living in small-town Texas, feels alienated from the person she knows she should be and would be if only she truly believed it possible. If Kenzi finds the ability to forgive her own mistakes and the mistakes of others, she may have a chance to meet her destiny head-on.

Things I Forgot to Tell You

Lee McQueen

Poetry Collection
ISBN 978-0-978515-3-7
2007
2nded.
Out of Print
Poems speak on uncertainty, sadness, despair, guilt, anger, frustration, love, hope, forgiveness, happiness, joy, and spirituality. Poetry is interactive. The reader or listener meets the author or speaker halfway and fills the poem with their own reality and expectations. A lot like life and diamonds, poetry reflects back an image that depends on where one stands in relation to the expressions.

Imaginarium

Lee McQueen

Short Story Collection
ISBN-13: 978-0979851506
2006

Fourteen short stories describe inner turmoil that drives change. Especially when the characters who inhabit the stories step outside the ordinary for a moment in time. And so, there remains the Imaginarium, where Dreamers know when to take a chance and Heroes know when to make a stand. Because refusing to make a choice is a choice. And sometimes, the least of all has the greatest ability to influence the future of the world.

www.ingramcontent.com/pod-product-compliance
Lightning Source LLC
Chambersburg PA
CBHW072021040426
42447CB00009B/1681